Critique and Utopia

Critique and Utopia

New Developments in the Sociology of Education in the Twenty-First Century

Edited by Carlos Alberto Torres and António Teodoro

ROWMAN & LITTLEFIELD PUBLISHERS, INC.
Lanham • Boulder • New York • Toronto • Plymouth, UK

ROWMAN & LITTLEFIELD PUBLISHERS, INC.

Published in the United States of America
by Rowman & Littlefield Publishers, Inc.
A wholly owned subsidiary of The Rowman & Littlefield Publishing Group, Inc.
4501 Forbes Boulevard, Suite 200, Lanham, Maryland 20706
www.rowmanlittlefield.com

Estover Road
Plymouth PL6 7PY
United Kingdom

British Library Cataloguing in Publication Information Available

Library of Congress Cataloging-in-Publication Data

Critique and utopia : new developments in the sociology of education in the twenty-first
century / edited by Carlos Alberto Torres and António Teodoro.
    p. cm.
  ISBN-13: 978-0-7425-3846-7 (cloth : alk. paper)
  ISBN-10: 0-7425-3846-X (cloth : alk. paper)
  ISBN-13: 978-0-7425-3847-4 (pbk. : alk. paper)
  ISBN-10: 0-7425-3847-8 (pbk. : alk. paper)
  1. Educational sociology. 2. Educational sociology—Research. I. Torres, Carlos
Alberto. II. Teodoro, António.
  LC191.C69 2007
  306.43—dc22   2006036687

Printed in the United States of America

∞™ The paper used in this publication meets the minimum requirements of American
National Standard for Information Sciences—Permanence of Paper for Printed Library
Materials, ANSI/NISO Z39.48-1992.

Steve Stoer: In Memoriam

The editors and contributors would like to dedicate this book to the loving memory of our dear friend and colleague, Steve Stoer, Professor *Catedrático* of the University of Porto, Portugal. Steve passed away the last day of the year 2005. With his untimely death, the sociology of education has lost one its most insightful, prolific, and imaginative practitioners. His intellectual contributions, brilliance, and warm personality will be sorely missed. Yet his message will continue to reverberate for years to come. He has taught us, and a whole generation of younger sociologists of education, that there should be no limits to the rigorous sociological imagination if one teaches and conducts research, as he did, not only to interpret but also to change the world.

Contents

1

Introduction

Critique and Utopia in the Sociology of Education

António Teodoro and Carlos Alberto Torres

The noted Argentinean writer Jorge Luis Borges once said that politics and fiction mesh together while simultaneously stealing mutually from each other; they are two universes at the same time symmetrical but irreconcilable.

This book invites us to carefully inspect the connections between fiction and politics in education, assessing the importance of the notion of utopia in the context of social theory and exploring new developments in the sociology of education.

Utopia is a term used here in the sense of philosopher Paul Ricoeur, as ucronia, that is, the symbolic representation of a time reconfigured by narrative fiction. In the realm of social sciences, Immanuel Wallerstein has resorted to a term he coined, utopistics, as a way to evaluate the historical choices of the twenty-first century.

> Utopistics is the serious assessment of historical alternatives, the exercise of our judgment as to the substantive rationality of alternative possible historical systems. It is the sober, rational, and realistic evaluation of human social systems, the constraints on what they can be, and the zones open to human creativity. Not the face of the perfect (and inevitable) future, but the face of an alternative, better, and historically possible (but far from certain) future.[1]

Utopistics is a useful term in the sociology of education discussion that addresses the crisis of schooling and determines whether the school system could eventually become an inclusive multicultural public sphere and what role education plays in the context of the process of globalization.[2] Utopistics could help us ascertain if education and schooling may help us to live together in justice and peace.

Given the enormous and ever-increasing tasks attributed to education in the Liberal Enlightenment[3]—from socialization and labor force training to developing creativity in science and technology, and to moral reasoning—not surprisingly, from its beginnings, the sociology of education has mostly focused on the process of schooling.

Despite practical difficulties and different rhythms of expansion, schools have been a central pillar of the process of internationalization of culture; some schools were already associated with the phenomenon of globalization and yet others were quite distinct from it.[4] Educational systems have widely expanded, almost isomorphically, throughout the world. The expansion rates, in terms of enrollment and public expenditures, particularly after World War II, matched if not surpassed the expansion of most other public social services. School systems have managed to include ever-growing sectors of the population. It is not uncommon to find that many families plan their daily lives around school calendars and requirements. Even more, with the changes surrounding the creation of the European Union, these calendars and institutional developments—including processes of accreditation that are compatible across borders—have became a continental experience.

In a sense, it is the consolidation of a massive, compulsory, state-administered, and financially sponsored educational system that has been one of the key instruments to fulfill a basic premise of the Enlightenment: enlightenment through the expansion of reason to all social strata.[5] Indeed, "The modern nation-state self-consciously uses language policy, formal education, collective rituals, and mass media to integrate citizens and ensure their loyalty."[6] This culturalist perspective[7] has systematically argued that through rituals linking individuals to society, and themselves to the state, the state has manipulated master narratives for national representations.

Since the inception of nation-states and particularly after 1945, a state's master narratives have attributed very peculiar roles to educational systems and particularly to teachers.[8] On the one hand, through massive, compulsory education, the state seems to offer a strategy of social mobility, training, and inclusion, which facilitates the lives of its citizens. On the other hand "it links citizens to one another and to the state, subverting other narratives and thus the possibility of other autonomous, authoritative narratives."[9] Finally, "the master narrative creates the limits and possibilities of the institutions involved in social control."[10]

From the perspective of the theories of social reproduction,[11] one may argue that the main model of massive education was progressively developed in Europe and the United States and expanded to the four corners of the world as the only possible and imaginable model of educating (and controlling) citizens. On the other hand, comparable educational reforms have taken place in socialist and capitalist societies alike under the principles of developing cognitive and moral reasoning, imparting official knowledge, facilitating social mobility, job training, or credentialism.

Yet, it would not have been imaginable that at the beginning of the twenty-first century, few other social institutions will be so harshly criticized as education, as so many educational experiences called into question: "never before [have] so many lost their trust in the schools; never before [have] so many tried to avoid schooling; never before [have] so many criticized education, and never before [have] so many people have doubts about the directions and appropriateness of school reforms."[12]

Surely, there have been challenges to schooling along the way, most prominently in the 1970s, in the realm of cultural studies with the proposal to de-schooling by Ivan Illich.[13] While Illich's proposal anticipated many of the new forms of teaching and learning which take place outside of the schools (for example, the Internet as a source of teaching and learning), it failed to criticize the principles, functions, and structures of educational systems—and eventually neglected to develop alternative institutional practices that might have worked in the transformation of such systems, both from the inside and from the perspective of social change and transformation of political systems.

Many of these criticisms are well-founded due to the serious tensions that exist in education worldwide. These tensions can be formulated in terms of Durkheim's functional analysis: schools provide both the socialization of children and youth (some European countries, the United States, Canada, and Japan have mandatory education for people under 18 years of age, hence reaching an enrollment and operational ceiling), and the educational base of the population as a whole (not only the youth, which is entering labor markets, but also the population at large, pursuing different professions in growingly specialized and diversified labor markets).

It is in this context that the dominant areas of specialization are chronologically divided into the following segments: preschool, elementary, secondary, higher education, and adult education, and all of them confront different yet related challenges. The tendency is to extend by law obligatory schooling to incorporate middle school (that is up to 17 or 18 years of age). This will definitely put more pressure on school environments and policies.

Another important challenge is the question of the appropriate curriculum for an age of globalization and high-technology cultures, what some journalists in the 1970s coined the emerging "knowledge society." Many scholars have criticized that during the second half of the twentieth century, schools were mostly parking lots, in which children and youths of the most diverse origins, cultures, genders, ethnicities, and different personal aspirations and talents, mingled aimlessly under the care of an educational bureaucracy while their parents worked. While this might still be the case in some places, schools also play a major role beyond their academic, cognitive, or moral functions: schools constitute one of the few sites of social solidarity where the poor people, a growing proportion of girls, and the immigrants receive school lunches and health care, since many other social systems provided by the state have been drastically downsized or privatized.

The overall tenor of the educational reform proposed by neoliberalism rests on the rule of markets and eventually the privatization of the educational enterprise.[14] The dominant neoliberal agenda for globalization in K–12 education includes a drive toward privatization and decentralization of public forms of education, a movement toward educational standards, a strong emphasis on testing, and a focus on accountability. Specific to higher education reform, neoliberal versions of globalization suggest reforms for universities in four primary areas: efficiency and accountability, accreditation and universalization, international competitiveness, and privatization.

These reforms, associated with international competitiveness, could be described as *competition-based reforms*. These reforms are characterized by efforts to create measurable performance standards through extensive standardized testing (the new standards and accountability movement), introduction of new teaching and learning methods leading to the expectations of better performance at low cost (e.g., universalization of textbooks), and improvements in the selection and training of teachers.

Competition-based reforms in higher education tend to adopt a vocational orientation and reflect the point of view that colleges and universities exist largely to serve the economic well-being of a society. With regard to accreditation and universalization, major worldwide efforts are under way to reform academic programs through accreditation processes and various strategies that produce increased homogeneity across national boundaries.

The privatization of higher education in debt-ridden countries such as Mexico, Brazil, and Argentina typically is advanced by the IMF and the World Bank as a precondition to further monetary lending to these countries. A precondition of such lending involves the transfer of educational financing from higher education to lower levels of education—on the premise that subsidizing higher education is in fact subsidizing the rich, since the majority of students enrolled in higher education are from middle-class and affluent families.

Needless to say, these reforms are actively resisted in some of these countries by faculties, unions, parents, social movements, and students. Indeed, globalization has had a major impact in education since international institutions have promoted finance-driven reforms that eventually clash with the possibility of equity-driven reforms in many countries.

By and large, public schools enroll students without openly discriminating in social, cultural, economic, or ethnic terms. Hence, educational reform is commonly signaled as society's tool to deal with most social problems—from the traditional problems resulting from poverty, unemployment, or class polarization in unequal societies, to the new problems that seem to affect industrialized and advanced societies, problems such as tabaquism, drug addition, sexually transmissible diseases and AIDS, or the social destruction of entire neighborhoods in large cities, oftentimes affected by the phenomena of social exclusion. Alan Touraine posed a most challenging question when he asked if we can live together. This is a pressing question for educational systems. Can schools and educational systems answer the needs of diverse cultures, diverse interests, diverse cognitive requirements, diverse labor markets, and globalized societies?[15]

These questions emerge as even more substantive when optimism is lacking in our societies. At the end of World War II, societies unleashed renewed democratic energy and a new world system was structured around nations, which parsimoniously but steadily began to abandon the colonialism of empires around a notion of international law—reflected in the creation of the United Nations as a source of legitimacy as much as a tool for conflict resolution. This epoch has been termed by Immanuel Wallerstein as "the American Peace."[16] The idea of the welfare state that emerges in the postwar period was one of renewed optimism because of economic growth (in Europe, Japan, and the United States), new models of economic assistance (both bilateral and multilateral), and a fervor in the process of modernization as a panacea in capitalist societies, to eliminate poverty, discrimination, and inequality. Paradoxically, the culmination of this Enlightenment ideal as a model of economic development merely accepted internationally has since further developed into the present model of economic, political, and sociocultural globalization. The nation-state became less relevant in the construction of policies and the global markets dancing to the tune of the Washington Consensus created a very different environment—one based on fiscal discipline and priorities for social expenditure, fiscal reform, financial liberalization, free trade, direct foreign investment, privatization, deregulation, and rights of property.

Can we live together in the context of these changes prompted by globalization? Can schools and educational systems answer these dilemmas? These are some of the topics discussed in this book, with particular attention to the recent contributions of sociological theory to the study of education facing the challenges of the twenty-first century.

We need utopistics, perhaps new utopias with a renewed sense of critique. Utopistics can guide the transformation of society and imagine a postneoliberal era—a transition that is emerging in directions difficult to predict. One thing is for sure: educational systems have a major role to play, and educational theory has major challenges ahead.

THE ORGANIZATION OF THIS BOOK

The book is divided in two main sections. The first one deals with perspectives and debates for the twenty-first century. The second one focuses on the new resources for the sociology of education.

Part I discusses the problematic of schooling in the context of globalization and the struggle for democracy. The contributions of Licínio C. Lima, Roger Dale, António M. Magalhães and Stephen R. Stoer, António Teodoro, and Clementina Marques Cardoso offer fresh European perspectives on these issues. From a North American viewpoint, David F. Suarez and Francisco O. Ramirez offer a systematic analysis of the rise of human rights in education.

In part II, we honor the tradition of sociological theory applied to education through contributions from Ana Maria Morais on Basil Bernstein; Jose Eustaquio Romão on Freire's pedagogy as a teaching for the sociology of education; Patricia M. McDonough and Anne-Marie Nuñez on Pierre Bourdieu; and Carlos Alberto Torres on Freire's theory of transformative social justice learning.

As scholars and as educators, we are convinced that the present cannot be the measure of happiness, because happiness is simply a collection of images that vanish with distance and become distorted with proximity. Yet, we are also convinced that a utopia is that horizon and, as the poet has defined, a horizon that as we take two steps to get closer to it, it moves two steps away. We take two more steps to get closer still, and it again moves two steps away. What is the use of utopia then, one may wonder. The answer is simply this: It helps us to walk, as Jose Luis Borges, in his insightful merging of politics and fiction, not only in the narratives but in practice, taught us.

NOTES

1. Immanuel Wallerstein. *Utopistics; Or Historical Choices in the Twenty-First Century.* (New York: The New Press, 1998), pp. 1–2.
2. British scholar David Held has argued that we live in a world that is a community of destiny, in which there is such an overlapping in our daily lives, that work, money, creeds, commerce, communications, finance, and even the environment are more interconnected every day. While observing that the signals in the current world

system are cause for preoccupation, he wants to remain optimistic that the gains in the international system since 1945 could be preserved.

Yet, he pinpoints four factors that may deeply affect the contemporary world: (1) the collapse of the regulation of the world trade, increasing the global inequality; (2) the lack of progress of the UN goal of the millennium to establish minimum humanitarian levels for ample sectors of the world population; (3) the failure to address global warming of the planet; and (4) the erosion of the multilateral order, as symbolized by the UN and extended to a series of international agreements and agencies. "Globalización: el peligro y la respuesta." *El Pais* (July 4, 2004), pp. 13–14.

3. We should take the arguments about the triumph of liberalism with a grain of salt, particularly when Immanuel Wallerstein has proposed the provocative thesis that "the collapse of the Communism represents not the final success of liberalism as an ideology but the decisive undermining of the ability of liberal ideology to continue its historical role." Wallerstein, *After Liberalism* (New York: The New Press, 1995), p. 3.

4. N. Burbules and C. A. Torres, eds., *Education and Globalization: Critical Analysis* (New York: Routledge, 2000).

5. Jürgen Habermas. *The Postnational Constellation: Political Essays* (Cambridge, MA: MIT Press, 2001). Translated, edited, and with an introduction by Max Pensky.

6. Michel Schudson, "Culture and Integrations of National Societies." *International Social Science Journal* 45 (February 1994): 64.

7. As an example, see the work of Clifford Geertz, *The Interpretation of Cultures: Selected Essays* (New York: Basic Books, 1973).

8. See Luiza Cortesao, *Ser Professor: um ofício em risco de extinção? Reflexões sobre prática educativa face à diversidade, no limiar do século XXI* (Oporto: Afrontamento); C. A. Torres et al. *Sindicatos magisteriales y política educativa* (Buenos Aires, Argentina: Confederación de Trabajadores de la Educación de la República Argentina [CTERA] 2000), mimeographed; C. A. Torres et al. *Educational Reform and the Role of Teachers' Union* (Seoul, Korea: Korean Education Research Institute, 1999), mimeographed in English and Korean; C. A. Torres et al. *Teachers Unions and the State* (Osaka, Japan: Japanese Teachers Unions, 1998), mimeographed in English and Japanese.

9. Joel S. Migdal, *State in Society: Studying How States and Societies Transform and Constitute One Another*. (New York: Cambridge University Press, 2001), p. 261.

10. Migdal, State in Society, p. 261.

11. Raymond Morrow and Carlos Alberto Torres, *Social Theory and Education: A Critique of Theories of Social and Cultural Reproduction*. (Albany, NY: State University of New York Press, 1995). Portuguese translation 1999, Spanish translation, 2003.

12. João Barroso, A escola como espaço público local. In A. Teodoro (org.) *Educar, Promover, Emancipar. Os contributos de Paulo Freire e Rui Grácio para uma Pedagogia emancipatória* (Lisbon: Edições Universitárias Lusófonas, p. 201–22, 2001). Our translation.

13. See Carlos Alberto Torres's chapter 11 in this book.

14. For a systematic analysis and critique of the process of privatization of higher education in the Americas, see Robert Rhoads and Carlos Alberto Torres, editors, *The University, State, and Market. The Political Economy of Globalization in the Americas* (Stanford, CA: Stanford University Press, 2006).

15. Alan Touraine, *Pourrons-nous vivre ensemble? Egaux et différents* (Paris: Fayard, 1997).

16. Immanuel Wallerstein, *After Liberalism* (New York: The New Press, 1995), pp. 176–206.

I

Sociology of Education

New Perspectives and Debates in the Twenty-First Century

2

Schooling for Critical Education

The Reinvention of Schools as Democratic Organizations

Licínio C. Lima

The state school, with a public status, independent from church and family, has historically represented an essential project to the constitution of modern societies, led under state control. The cultural and symbolic emergence of the nation-state concept and the respective national citizenship has also partly derived from the socializing action of that new formal organization, that is, the public school.

Like most of the formally and artificially constructed modern organizations, provided with purposes, objectives, structures, resources, and technologies, school as a public formal organization has shifted, within a century, from the condition of a novelty looking for consolidation to the status of a strongly institutionalized and omnipresent reality. The institutionalization process of school organization and organized pedagogic action, which occurred in the *longue durée*, had as a consequence the expansion of the state school and its naturalization, as if it were a biologically spread phenomenon, naturally disseminated and consequently taken for granted since then.

However, the ideas of either an original model of schooling (probably deriving from an embryologic and ahistorical metaphor) or a primordial model of schooling (which would concentrate a kind of universal dimension of formal organization), or still the sociotechnical logic based on the structural and morphological requirements of a given pedagogical technology (based on class teaching), are nothing but poor arguments to justify the success and expansion of a certain political and institutional school model.

Even the recent identification of several "isomorphisms" in the process of "worldwide dissemination of school"—which have been pointed by some neoinstitutionalist theses revealing standard patterns following an educational globalization which might derive from a *common educational culture* (Meyer,

2000)—runs the risk, as Roger Dale remarked (2001), of depoliticizing the issue, of concealing both the action of economic and political forces and new powers on a global scale, in building global educational agendas.

As Max Weber had concluded, based on his cultural pessimism, the universes of formal organization have become indispensable for the legitimacy and reproduction of new forms of domination, based on a rational, legal authority. The schooling process, as a state political strategy and typical form of citizen education in the modern nation-state, could only be achieved through a process of organizational formalization. On the other hand, formal organization would constitute an indispensable tool, not only in the search for effectiveness—and *being modern means being effective*, as reminded by Stewart Clegg (1990)—but also in the perpetuation of power.

Observing the political dimensions of the organizational and administrative phenomena is essential in order to avoid atomized and instrumental conceptions of school organization. State schools are a social and historical construction, deeply dependent on the different contexts and the political, economic, and cultural forces that recognize themselves as dominant ones. In spite of being institutionalized from the normative standpoint, the education process through state schools is far from imposing itself efficiently on a planetary scale. Its expansion process, considered remarkable by many, is far from it, not only in geographical but also in socioeconomic and cultural terms. Anyway, this process is neither linear nor irreversible and, on the contrary, the idea of state schools is currently much less consensual and much more problematic than in the recent past, in many cases finding itself under siege and the object of social policies based on privatization, deregulation, or devolution.

The so-called crisis in state schools does not present itself as an essentially educational or pedagogical crisis; it is also a crisis ideologically built through an ideological discourse that, as Marilena Chauí defends (1990: 3), "is the one that aims at coinciding with things." By deriving from different political projects and from distinct agendas and mandates for education, school crisis seems inevitable, although, as it is understood, only partially affirmed as a crisis of schooling. In any case, it is not my belief this is simply a crisis in the schooling organization model—as if such a model really existed in a universal and singular way, as absolutely standardized and indifferent to contexts, history, and politics.

A school version of the end of history, in the style of Francis Fukuyama, celebrating not only the end of ideologies and the overcoming of the concept of social class, but also the absolute triumph of a given school model, would not just represent the total failure of many historical attempts to democratize school education and strengthen democratic citizenship, through the contributions of a critical schooling. Such a setting would already represent a final solution to the crisis, destroying any glimmer of hope in the possibility of reinventing schools as democratic organizations, through the only process known: the exercise of the active citizenship in the context of democratic struggles for social democratization.

The schooling process for a critical education, on its own, is far from being able to guarantee the required democratization of democracy. However, it is no doubt vital to confront the one that is probably the most serious crisis the state schools have experienced so far—a crisis in its public vocation, which is neither much mentioned nor publicly discussed, relieving the schools of any idea of social responsibility and improvement, solidarity, and civic and moral commitment toward the full education of the public.

THE FORMAL ORGANIZATION OF SCHOOLING: THE TAYLORIZATION OF INSTRUCTION AND THE PERPETUATION OF CONTROL

The edification of the modern school as an organization specialized in providing knowledge and especially in socializing children and youngsters (according to Emile Durkheim's definition) has followed the most typical guidelines of the modernity and capitalism organizational ideologies. In search of the optimal relation between means and ends and of "the one best way" principle, the education system has adopted a productivist and instrumental feature, fragmenting the school curriculum and "taylorizing" the process of instruction. Besides, the defense of mass production, labor division, and optimization in a school context has even preceded the praise of the division of labor by Adam Smith, for whom education would be the essential institution to fight against the alienation resulting from the technical division of labor. On his *Didactica Magna*, Comenius had already proposed those principles of *organizational modernization*, promising a universal art to teach everything to everyone and everywhere.

Time and space control, specialization and fragmentation, separation of design and implementation, and the concepts of order and discipline represent some of the rationalist and mechanist items that could already be identified in nineteenth-century religious schools, even before the expansion of the state school. As with the origin of the manufacturing plant, the education system seminally carries a project of power and control that only superficially could justify its structural and morphological options in terms of a radical change of the organizational technology, that is, of the pedagogical process of transmission. Such dimensions of domination, hierarchical order, and centralized control were rather appreciated by Frederick Taylor, who observed them with

interest as schooling characteristics and recognized their usefulness to industrial organization, under the principles of "scientific management." As reminded by the Brazilian sociologist Maurício Tragtenberg (2002: 11):

> At school, being watched, looked at, counted in detail becomes a means of con-
> trol, domination, a method to document individualities. Creating that documen-
> tary field has allowed the entrance of the individual into the field of knowledge
> and, logically, a new type of power has emerged over the bodies.

It is this genealogy, both political and technical-rational, of state schools that
allows us to understand the success obtained in the dissemination of a formal
organization geared to mass production from a process of taylorization of instruction. This system would thus assure a high productivity and efficiency
and also the perpetuation of state control over families, community, and education professionals. For this reason, although the school organizational
structures and morphology are not indifferent, they are far from fully representing the traditional school organizational model. This model—empirically
implemented through a plurality of options and, in practice, manifesting itself
in a large diversity of organizational models in action (cf. Lima, 2003:
93–114)—mainly involves a certain philosophy, a prevailing *Weltanschau-
ung*, political options and interests, and a project of control assisted by
techno-bureaucracy. Thus, a specific school organizational model is also, and
perhaps mainly, the policy, values, and objectives that shape the structures
represented on the formal structure, that justify technologies and production
processes as the best or satisfactory means, and that give meaning to organizational action. As there is no political action without organization and mobilization, every organizational action is, by definition, a political one, too.

   As for schooling, there would be no schooling institution without organizational expression and materialization. But this does not mean that the
choice of a mechanized and bureaucratic design of organization, as well as
the option on a nondemocratic organization, geared to control, may be considered as natural or without alternative. The organizational *design*, in spite
of its technical dimensions, is mainly a political action. The "politicization"
of education, conceptualized by Paulo Freire, certainly includes school organization and its governance. In spite of launching one of the most lucid and
violent attacks on traditional school and "banking" education, exponents of
the bureaucratic organization and technical and instrumental rationality in education, Freire (*Pedagogy of the Oppressed*, 1972) never gave up or re-
nounced the fight for the democratization of education. By rejecting the
school political and axiological neutrality, he also rejected depoliticized conceptions of school organization and, simultaneously, political and educational
conceptions deprived of its organizational and administrative dimensions.

Like other critical pedagogues, he does not ignore how the organizational apparatuses have historically served domination projects and have evaded democracy and citizenship, supporting the reproduction of authoritarian powers. Recognizing it, however, does not restrain him from refusing the immanent, natural, or suprahistorical character of the organizational domination, as if the organizational phenomena were intrinsically antidemocratic, a kind of iron law of oligarchy, or of sectarianism of revolutionary vanguards, which would eliminate every possibility of social change and defeat, a priori and without any need for fight, or any attempt to democratize formal organizations. That is, denying the possibility of a more democratic, free, and self-determined society and school.

On the contrary, *the organization as a practice of freedom*, based on the exercise of participative democracy also within formal organizations, is indispensable to political and social democratization and to the emergence of citizens as autonomous democratic individuals, not mere well-informed subjects or consumers. As far as school is concerned, it is convenient not to ignore that its modes of organization and governance also constitute themselves as implicit pedagogy and hidden curriculum—through actions, neither neutral nor merely instrumental, which promote values, organize and regulate a social context where people socialize and are socialized, and where rules are produced and reproduced and powers are exercised. Here lies one of the major potentials for democracy, autonomy, and human rights development; although in full contradiction with the bureaucratic, instrumental, and control feature historically imposed on it. However, it will suffice to compare state schools to most of social and formal organizations of our time to find the potentially relevant differences that still exist. With all its contradictions, state schools represent to large social contingents of students the organization with more democratic rules, with a more humane and warmer environment, and with a less competitive and selective ethos, which they will hardly find again in the future. Nevertheless, this "treasure" to be found and reinforced is particularly demanding in terms of autonomy of the pedagogical subjects and of the pedagogical work, requiring its re-significance and avoiding the alienation of teachers and students.

Reinventing school as a nonalienated workplace, that is, "dealienating school work" (Canário, 2002: 150), represents a démarche essential to the project of democratizing school and its mode of governance.

As Tragtenberg (2002: 16) defended in a paper on power relations at school:

The possibility of separating knowledge from power, at [the] school level, resides in the creation of horizontal structures where teachers, students, and other school staff constitute a real community. This outcome can only derive from many struggles, sectoral victories, and also defeats. But self-governing schools ruled by education staff—including the students—is a condition for school democratisation.

THE CRISIS OF THE INCOMPETENT SCHOOL:
ADAPTATION AND PERFORMANCE

The unfulfilled promises of modern school concerning the democratization of knowledge, the fight against social inequalities and the development of freer and more autonomous citizens, hindered by the contradictions between modernization and development, between regulation and emancipation, and between heteronomy and autonomy, partly coincide with the unfulfilled promises of modernity. Although this is no doubt a critical area where the state school has revealed its incompetence, it is convenient, on the other hand, to avoid naive pedagogism. As Geoff Whitty (2002: 124) warns, "blaming schools for the problems of society is both unfair and unproductive [. . .]. Schools can certainly make a difference, but they cannot buck social trends on their own."

Schools cannot stop being held responsible for the pursuit, or not, of the objectives of a democratic education, which presuppose actions and procedures toward building a school as a democratic organization and as an organization promoting democracy. But the democratization of schools is far from being just a school problem or, mainly, a technical and pedagogical problem. On the other hand, it seems very difficult to contribute to the constitution of the democratic citizen—a core political and pedagogical problem in the theory of participative democracy—discarding "schools as democratic public spheres" (Torres, 2001: 36, 288–89). As Morrow and Torres (1997: 147) consider that "the constitution of a democratic citizen implies the creation of a pedagogical subject," they note that establishing the latter represents, in fact "a core conceptual problem, a democracy dilemma."

The mass production of citizens, through standardized processes and under centralized, nondemocratic, and heteronomous control, represents a fatal contradiction. Education toward democratic citizenship cannot be attained by means of organizational structures, of control and leadership forms, of schooling processes and pedagogical methods—all precisely characterized by their lack of democratic commitment. However, democracy, solidarity, and common good still represent the major problems of state schools. As discourse and practice, as method and content, democracy remains significantly absent from school. This is truly the most critical face of a state school minimally committed to the democratic education of the public.

In the past, the absence of democracy occurred when it was, rhetorically, considered as a core significant value and its effective achievement would then be a synonym of the efficiency of social policies of progressive and social-democratic inspiration, typical of the welfare state. It concerned a guideline based on the public provision of education, on the facilitation of access and on the guarantee of equal opportunities, through social policies centered on the state's redistributive role and on the government's responsibility for the promulgation of educational policies and the regulation of the sector, by means of prescriptive legislation. Nevertheless, although we should recognize the expansion of public schooling and a larger democratization in its access, consistent with a conception of education toward democracy and social responsibility, it is convenient not to ignore the technocratic drifts, guided by more pragmatic and functional objectives and inspired by modernization and human capital theories. The expansion of cultural and social rights through state schools would once again reveal itself in deep tension with the bureaucratic and centralized state control and with the meritocratic and discriminatory dimensions of public policies that claimed to be democratic and equalitarian. So, I believe Whitty is correct when he states:

> Even if the social democratic era looks better in retrospect, and in comparison with neoliberal policies, than it did at the time, that does not remove the need to rethink what might be progressive policies for the new century. (2002: 21)

Now, democracy remains absent from school and from the dominant public discourses on education. Consequently, its effective accomplishment would tend to be identified as an irrational and ineffective organization, paralyzed by retrograde objectives of social improvement, to the detriment of innovation, competitiveness, adaptation, and performance—typical of the economic rationality and of flexible labor imperative in new capitalism. Social improvement, democracy, and solidarity give way to individual performance and competitiveness. The educational thinking itself seems now much more permeable to the theses of management and economy gurus (like Peter Drucker and Michael Porter, among others) and to the theories of "public choice" and "new public management."

As a matter of fact, the "neoliberal welfare reform model of social policy" (Griffin, 1999) changed the focus from the provision of education by the state to the status of learning cultures and to the concept of learning, which is more individualistic, fragmented, and instrumental in nature. By emphasizing a more functional and adaptive concept of learning and overlooking the fact that, ultimately, there is no life without learning, they run the risk of dissolving the substantiveness of life throughout the learning process and abandoning the goals of transformation of both individual and collective life, in all its dimensions.

The reformist principles of neoliberal inspiration advocate a minimal role for the state and a leading one for society and the market. They are based on the concept of choice in accordance with the most typical individual (and competitive) strategies and rationalities which suit the lifestyles, interests, and needs of the clients and consumers of education. The strategic search for learning opportunities—which are transformed into "competitive advantages"—is now an individual responsibility. It becomes an object of choice and the individual has to accept the consequences of good and bad choices, success or failure in the job market, and of his/her (in)ability to determine and forecast optimal training routes. The individual will thereby design a rational learning biography that will purportedly produce high levels of employability, competitiveness, adaptability, and mobility. As if it were possible in those that Ulrich Beck (1992) defined as "risk societies," to guarantee a constant, isomorphic, and successful adaptation to social change, from a paradigm of individual learning, capable of acting as an all risks insurance, taken out by someone who is represented as useful, alone, highly competitive, and performative.

But school has been considered incompetent and in crisis whenever the adaptation to economy and competitive performance is not at the core of its mission. Learning humanity, solidarity, and common good have perished with the status of modernist antiques in the light of a pedagogy against the other. *Formativity*, critically defined by Basil Bernstein (2001: 14) as the individual ability the actor should have, only reveals its effectiveness when used against the other, with less "competence to compete." But, contrary to what is stated by the dominant vocationalist ideologies, a school that would be able to fully satisfy the economic demands and needs, producing the profiles and competences that are presented as imperatives, would be condemned to collapse. The competitive advantages and individual improvement would then be shared by everyone, or by the majority of individuals, being no longer advantageous and competitive. They would irrevocably be replaced with new requirements, more selective and statistically less distributed within the respective population.

In practice, however, this ideology can impute responsibility for unemployment on the school and its inefficiency in the production of skills society considers as relevant. It does so by hiding the economic and managerial rationale, which justify unemployment as a solution and conceive the downsizing phenomena as economic rationalization and entrepreneurial modernization strategies. The concept of employability, a symbol of the "conservative exaltation of individual responsibility" that changes each individual agent into an "*entrepreneur de lui-même*," as Bourdieu (2001: 28) denounced, represents now one of the largest political and pedagogical mystifications that influences state schools and that shapes curriculum, pedagogical practice, and assessment. As István Mészáros (2003: 121) has recently explained, following his defense of society *beyond capital*, the fight against massive structural unemployment, under the labor concept of "a quantifiable cost of production," is absolutely inconsequent.

However, in "liquid modernity," according to Zygmunt Bauman (2001: 141), "the art of administration [. . .] consists of keeping the 'human labour force' away or, even better, making it withdraw." The short time, the immediate and instantaneous, became dominant, adopting the logic of consumption and choice without thinking of the long run. It is this apology of "nothing in the long run" that, according to Richard Sennett (2001: 37), "corrodes trust, loyalty and mutual commitment" consequently engendering the need for a schooling geared to flexibility and perhaps even for the "corrosion of character," through potentially corrosive pedagogical practices, but not educational anymore.

It is in this precise field of the schooling process, from conceptions and policies that "destroy the common good," adopting the "values and criteria typical of the capitalist market economy," according to Ricardo Petrella (2002: 19), that school reveals again its great potential. A renewed social agency, with centuries of experience, is now forced to convert its action against the existence of the other, defined as a natural enemy. A school orientated toward the best, the fittest and most competent, the strongest and the winner, is a school specialized in conquering; that is, a privileged tool of socialization against common good.

If it is true, as Stephen Stoer (2002: 43) has recently sustained, that "companies, associations, social, political, religious movements and the family itself, etc., already present themselves explicitly in some countries as alternatives to state school," it is however necessary to know to which social groups and classes, and in what dimensions of the schooling process, these alternatives have emerged. Nevertheless, I have serious doubts about the loss of the school centrality as a socializing agency, mentioned by Stoer on the same text. On the contrary, educational reforms have put school at the core of the attacks against the social-democratic policies and made it the driving force of the change they wish to achieve. Subjected to scrutiny and under immense pressure from governments, mass media, and public opinion, school has not only acquired an excessive protagonism in the last years (as if the future of society and economy would mainly depend on its performance), but also served as a model to a broader schooling process of pedagogical social problems. To this purpose, António Nóvoa (2002: 244) considers the appeal to education and lifelong learning as "the most recent episode of the society schooling long process" and Bernstein (2001: 13), referring to the United

Kingdom, stated that there were more and more proofs of what he called the "Totally Pedagogised Society."

What seems to be occurring is a pandemic propagation of certain, typical school dimensions to social and economic spheres. Simultaneously, there is a process to fight for the control of the school socialization functions and respective values and objectives, which are under an accelerated mutation process.

The "treasure" has already been found by the neoliberal and neoconservative policies—school is too important as an agent of transmission and socialization to be subjected to democracy and solidarity ideals, that is, engaged in a political culture in "countercurrent in societies where the possessive and mercantilistic individualism prevails" (Santos, 2002: 120). The school system's institutional survival does not seem to be at stake. What is at stake is a democratic conception of state schools, especially when certain social classes refuse to support it and, many times, refuse to send their children. As Stephen Ball (2003: 21) has recently concluded, one of the effects of the market and competitiveness logic "has been a loss of support among the new middle class for efforts to democratize education and social policy and the progressive experimentation in educational methods and pedagogies."

That is why the democratic reinvention of school seems to be the only possible affirmative answer to the question Could schooling be another thing?

THE REINVENTION OF SCHOOLS AS DEMOCRATIC ORGANIZATIONS

I do not believe it is possible to design, in advance and in detail, a democratic school—in an exercise of technocratic and demiurgic enlightenment—which would immediately deny the necessarily democratic character of its constitution process. In this case, it is not a question of "finding" democratic schools, but rather of beginning the process of their collective reinvention and construction. Policy, values, and objectives represent again nuclear elements that will give meaning to the organizational design, curriculum, and assessment—the specific pedagogical practices in specific contexts of action. So, therefore, the classic idea of a single model of organization and governance, singular and uniform, probably legitimated by a new type of "the one best way," even if it has now a democratic character, is not acceptable.

A school able to think about the present critically and to imagine the future creatively, contributing to its fulfilment through the political engagement in public causes and educational action committed to common good and the collective destiny of humankind, can only be a deliberative and autonomous school, of subjects who produce rules. A school should be inhabited by "moral actors" and not by "bystanders," according to Bauman's criticism (2002), actively pursuing social transformation and not a mere adaptation. Human emancipation, which Bauman believes currently means "the task of changing the de jure autonomy into a de facto autonomy" (2001: 62), cannot leave out the action of a more democratic and autonomous school. It is a question of the construction—surely slow and difficult but also possible—of a more democratic public, even without losing the state condition, and more autonomous and deliberative school, in spite of refusing the paradigm of the private entrepreneurial organization.

The school should be understood as public sphere and locus of co-governance between state, local community, and school actors. The state keeps the essential functions of provision, allocation, and redistribution of resources, as well as the generic definition of a common educational policy; but it decentralizes politically and relegitimizes democratically by giving back important decision powers to the former schooling peripheries. They, in turn, affirm themselves from now on as more central and configure a polycentric system endowed with a democratic governance. It is a question of a democratic devolution of self-government powers rather than a devolution of charges, abandoning public school to the mercy of market. This means that the concepts of autonomy, decentralization, and participation should be understood as being in rupture with the neoliberal semiotic process, which has been occurring for the last few decades. On the contrary, and resuming Paulo Freire's proposals on "changing the school face," which I studied in depth (cf. Lima, 2002), educational decentralization, school autonomy, and democratic participation assume a political and civic meaning inconsistent with managerial and neoscientific connotations. Decentralization and participation are not mere efficient management techniques toward rationalization and optimization. Autonomy, reduced to the decision on technical and operational dimensions, becomes a mere praise to the diversity of ways of peripheric implementation of the decisions centrally defined by central power. Such a system would be merely an autonomy where we are all just "autonomous" to creatively implement the decisions that others have already made for us. The democratic governance of school necessarily refers to a concept of ruling school, that is, to the idea of self-government and to a conception of autonomy as legitimate "power" in the process of decision making, in which, paraphrasing Freire, the transforming structures are subjects of their own transformation. A more democratic school is, by definition, a more autonomous and participative school. But participation is not functionally subordinate to the others' management act; it is not a fictional and heteronomous participation, but rather a participation in the decision-making process, as a free and responsible exercise of autonomous subjects. Only in this way will it be possible to teach and learn and to decide through the decision and participation practice, "experiencing the advantages and disadvantages of democratic adventure" (Freire, 1997: 18).

Nevertheless, school democratization does not represent just an educational and pedagogical problem. Being certain that it is an objective that cannot do without the intervention of school actors, it also seems clear that it is unachievable exclusively from its initiative. First, because the interests and rationalities in presence cannot be reduced to a single agenda. Plural and contradictory, the educational projects with expression at school level are by definition political-educational projects, reflecting and questioning values and guidelines of a wide range and circulation in society. To grasp this political nature of education and school is essential to the process of its democratic re-politization. School is not a mere instrument (*organon*) orientated according to the principles of *rational choice theory*, as if it were a question of a politically and axiologically neutral body.

As for teachers specifically, if they conscientiously assume the political and ethical dimensions that indelibly mark the pedagogical practices, the curriculum and assessment, the school organization, and its governance mode, they will hardly stop assuming themselves as political and pedagogical actors. This way they might open themselves to reflection, debate, and joint action with other actors, traditionally represented as external to school. They might link up with other bases of knowledge and power and find new support and alliances with social movements, nongovernmental organizations, community projects, and so forth. Then there will not be any need to deny their professionalism, to disregard their skilled pedagogical knowledge, or to give up their socioeducational interests, which, on the contrary, might condemn them to logics of adaptation to or capitulation on projects they consider unacceptable in democratic terms. But, on the other hand, it remains important to teachers to avoid entrenching themselves in closed universes of all types—technical, corporate, or bureaucratic—from which it is impossible to open education to public debate with nonmembers and nonexperts, or decentralize school and redirect it to debates on democracy and public interest.

Without running the risk of opening to a more extended community and social participation and to the exercise of a critical citizenship, becoming increasingly public, a school can hardly find allies in nonadministratively subordinate projects and stands. Reciprocal benefits are key as new allies should be able to engage themselves in the defense of education, joining efforts with school actors to amplify their pedagogical voices. To create a democratic school without the active participation of teachers and students is unthinkable; its achievement also requires the democratic participation of other sectors and the exercise of critical citizenship by other social actors—it is thus a task that can only be achieved in co-construction. It is my belief that if teachers and students remain isolated, they will hardly succeed in the democratization of educational powers and in the transformation of the school governance structures. Such objectives require sharing the power of decision over education, making decisions *with* others and not only *on* others, trying to build collectively free, fair, and democratic structures and rules, and creating a more inventive and manageable future on the part of the educational actors. Participating thus in the construction of an *opus proprium* and not just in the reproduction of an *opus alienum*, that is, co-building a democratic school and producing policies and rules in a regime of co-authorship.

Despite the difficulties and obstacles that a democratization project of educational powers will certainly face, a publicly critical education, committed to the de facto autonomy of society and its members, does not seem achievable without the democratic reinvention of schools as political and multicultural sites.

REFERENCES

Ball, Stephen J. (2003). *Class Strategies and the Education Market: The Middle Classes and Social Advantage*. London: RoutledgeFalmer.

Bauman, Zygmunt (2001). *Modernidade Líquida*. Rio de Janeiro: Jorge Zahar Editor.

——— . (2002). *Society under Siege*. Cambridge, MA: Polity Press.

Beck, Ulrich (1992). *Risk Society: Towards a New Modernity*. London: Sage.

Bernstein, Basil (2001). Das pedagogias aos conhecimentos. *Educação, Sociedade & Culturas* 15, 9–17.

Bourdieu, Pierre (2001). *Contre-feux 2 Pour un Mouvement Social Européen*. Paris: Raisons d'Agir.

Canário, Rui (2002). "Escola—Crise ou Mutação?" in *Espaços de Educação, Tempos de Formação*. Lisboa: Fundação Calouste Gulbenkian, 141–51.

Chauí, Marilena (1990). *Cultura e Democracia: O Discurso Competente e Outras Falas*. São Paulo: Cortez, 5th ed.

Clegg, Stewart R. (1990). *Modern Organizations: Organizational Studies in the Postmodern World*. London: Sage.

Dale, Roger (2001). Globalização e educação: demonstrando a existência de uma "cultura educacional mundial comum" ou localizando uma "agenda globalmente estruturada para a educação"? *Educação, Sociedade & Culturas* 16, 133–69.

Freire, Paulo (1972). *Pedagogy of the Oppressed*. Harmondsworth, UK: Penguin Books.

——— . (1997). *Professora Sim, Tia Não. Cartas a Quem Ousa Ensinar*. São Paulo: Olho d'Água.

Griffin, Colin (1999). Lifelong learning and welfare reform. *International Journal of Lifelong Education* 18, no. 6, 431–52.

Lima, Licínio C. (2002). *Organização Escolar e Democracia Radical. Paulo Freire e a Governação Democrática da Escola Pública.* São Paulo: Cortez/Instituto Paulo Freire, 3rd ed.

——. (2003). *A Escola como Organização Educativa. Uma Abordagem Sociológica.* São Paulo: Cortez, 2nd ed.

Mészáros, István (2003). Economia, política e tempo disponível: para além do capital. *Margem Esquerda—Ensaios Marxistas* 1, 93–124.

Meyer, John W. (2000). "Globalização e Currículo: problemas para a teoria em Sociologia da Educação" in *A Difusão Mundial da Escola*, ed. António Nóvoa & Jürgen Schriwer. Lisboa: Educa, 15–32.

Morrow, Raymond Allen, and Carlos Alberto Torres (1997). *Teoria Social e Educação: Uma Crítica da Reprodução Social e Cultural.* Porto: Afrontamento.

Nóvoa, António (2002). "O espaço público da educação: Imagens, narrativas e dilemas" in *Espaços de Educação: Tempos de Formação.* Lisboa: Fundação Calouste Gulbenkian, 237–63.

Petrella, Ricardo (2002). *O Bem Comum: Elogio da Solidariedade.* Porto: Campo das Letras.

Santos, Boaventura de Sousa (2002). *Democracia e Participação: O Caso do Orçamento Participativo de Porto Alegre.* Porto: Afrontamento.

Sennett, Richard (2001). *A Corrosão do Carácter: As Consequências Pessoais do Trabalho no Novo Capitalismo.* Lisboa. Teorema.

Stoer, Stephen R. (2002). Educação e globalização: entre regulação e emancipação. *Revista Crítica de Ciências Sociais* 63, 33–45.

Torres, Carlos Alberto (2001). *Democracia, Educação e Multiculturalismo. Dilemas da Cidadania em um Mundo Globalizado.* Petrópolis: Vozes.

Tragtenberg, Maurício (2002). "Relações de poder na Escola" in *Política e Gestão da Educação*, ed. Dalila Oliveira and Maria de Fátima Rosar. Belo Horizonte: Autêntica, 11–16.

Whitty, Geoff (2002). *Making Sense of Education Policy: Studies in the Sociology and Politics of Education.* London: Paul Chapman Publishing.

3

Globalization and the Rescaling of Educational Governance

A Case of Sociological Ectopia

Roger Dale

The chapter subtitle attempts to play on the theme of *utopia*, literally meaning "a good place" with a reference to an institution that is increasingly seen to have been "dis-placed," analytically and empirically. The institution is, of course, the state, and the burden of the chapter will be to examine the nature and plausibility of the "ectopic" state thesis as it might be seen in and contribute to the governance of education.

In this chapter, I argue first that the basis of the sovereign, autonomous national state, which the sociology of education has very largely taken for granted, has been severely eroded over the course of the past two decades. I suggest that one particular consequence of the erosion of the basis of the Keynesian Welfare National State (Jessop 1999) has been the generation of considerable confusion over the question of the "governance" of education systems, where the assumption that governance was the province solely of the state has been challenged from a number of directions. I also show conceptually what is involved in these shifts and consider what they may mean for educational policy and practice. The central argument is that changes in the governance of education are what I call *indirect effects* of the congeries of changes—in a range of spheres and at a number of levels—that are typically referred to as *globalization*. I will suggest that these changes have important theoretical consequences for the relationships among governance, regulation, and sovereignty, and will finally attempt to suggest some possible empirical outcomes of these changes.

Three broad points are essential to this argument. First, the nation-state basis of sociology of education, with its equation of (national) state and (national) society, needs to be problematized; in particular, the state has to become explanandum—itself to be explained—rather than remaining explanans—itself the explanation. Second, these changes will not lead to convergence between national education systems; while there may be appreciable sharing of educational agendas, these agendas will continue to be addressed in nationally specific ways, within the limits of what is a new functional and scalar division of the labor of educational governance. Third, I shall argue that in parallel with and associated with, rather than as a consequence of, these changes, we may begin to see quite significant changes in the patterns and purposes of educational reform, which seek to change the parameters of such reform rather than to improve education's performance within its "traditional" parameters.

Another effective subtitle for this chapter would have been "the state and education policy since 1989," and in a very real sense this might be seen as an attempt to revisit the book that I published in 1989, *The State and Education Policy*. In retrospect—and certainly not by intention or foresight—1989 proved to be a very appropriate year to publish that book. What happened internationally in 1989 represented the culmination of the kinds of states and education policies whose relationship over the previous forty-five years the book had aimed to understand. The assumptions of that book were in their main features what Bob Jessop has called the KWNS. In particular, while the book recognized that states were affected in major ways by their economic and political contexts, it was still possible to assume a relatively autonomous national state, with very considerable discretion, authority, and control over its education policy. The term *globalization* did not appear in the book, though due recognition was paid to the importance of the capitalist world economy, the international system of states and international organizations as carriers of the capitalist world economy (see also Dale 1992). In particular, the conception of a national economy, on which a national welfare state could depend for support, and which was embedded in a unique set of national institutions, had ceased to be valid.

Even though many of the events have been played out and many of the education policy purposes, processes, and outcomes are quite different from those of the earlier period, the fundamental arguments of the book remain valid—centering around the core problems of the capitalist state, the *social settlement*, and the relationships between the state, economy, and civil society. Of course, the forms of those sets of institutions and of those relationships may have changed. The most significant difference between the two eras is that the *national state* assumption of the earlier era that informed and was assumed by the book is no longer valid in a number of ways.

In terms of the core problems, the argument was that they derive from the extra-economic conditions of accumulation that capital itself is not capable of producing. These are supporting the accumulation process—for example, compensating for market failure in the provision of infrastructure; ensuring, by means of their monopoly of the legitimate use of violence, and of law-making capacity, a level of social order necessary for the stability of the society as a whole; and legitimating both the outcomes of the state's own activities and the means through which they are achieved.

However, the significance of their 'national' base for education systems extends beyond their role in guaranteeing the extra economic conditions. This is because education systems are the key institutions through which *societal cohesion* is achieved. This reflects a distinct element of state monopoly and uniqueness, for the state is the only institution within a society that is both responsible for, and able to bring about, societal cohesion. By societal cohesion, I mean not simply *social cohesion*, central though this is to societal cohesion. Social cohesion is in considerable part a function of the success of the state's discharge of its legitimation problem—the outcomes and processes of the distribution of prosperity and well-being. What societal cohesion adds to this is, on the one hand, a sense of a shared community of fate—in the sense of both protection from external and internal sources of risk. On the other hand, it brings a sense of national identity—both in terms of an appreciation of the "logic of appropriateness" of the means through which these outcomes are achieved (for instance, conceptions of democratic process) and of how they relate to and define who "we" are. Here, national education systems are the means through which (often-competing) narratives of nation are elaborated and confirmed. There is also something about *societal cohesion* that is reflected in the discussions about the place and importance of *social capital* [Fukuyama (1995), Putnam (2002), but also Fine (2001)], that is somehow intrinsic to a society and that cannot be externally induced or brought into being. It is not something that can be taught.

In terms of the changes to the social settlement, the changes that have occurred are most effectively and succinctly captured in Bob Jessop's KWNS/SWPR. Jessop (1999) points to a shift from the

Keynesian (state intervention in national economies through the control of demand levels in particular)

Welfare (state responsibility for ensuring redistribution of economic rewards)

National (based on the assumption of a national economy)

State (where the state/public sector was expected to be the provider as well as the funder of decommodified public services)

to the

Schumpeterian (state providing minimal and supporting conditions for the economy rather than directly intervening)

Workfare (responsibility for welfare individualized, with residual safety net)

Postnational (signaling a transnational economy in which the role and size of national economies were greatly diminished)

Regime (signaling that the state was only part of the apparatus through which societies were run and services delivered).

Alongside this account run arguments of the "hollowing out of the state," with some former responsibilities shifted upwards to the supranational level and others shifted downwards to subnational levels and to civil society. And finally, there seems to be some agreement that a hierarchical state model — with national states exercising unchallenged and exclusive control over their populations — no longer accurately accounts for the nature of the state's activity.

DEFINING GOVERNANCE

In defining my approach to *governance*, let us contrast it to three other views that seem to be prominent. The first of these sees governance as an alternative means of coordination to "state" and "market," where both are perceived to have failed. This perception is representative of several approaches that take governance as a more desirable or comfortable midpoint between the equally unpopular state and market forms. In this sense, it has clear affinities with the appeals to "network" or "civil society," or any of a host of equivalent terms that have been redeployed in different areas of the social sciences. The second use of governance takes it as denoting a particular form of technical response to the problems of public administration generated by the changes in the nature of the national state. Here, governance refers to processes through which some degree of administrative coherence, efficiency and effectiveness might be achieved. We see this in two forms — as the application of New Public Management at a national level and as a means of installing some kind of supranational governance, where, for instance, the phrase "governance without government" is invoked (Rosenau and Cziempel 1992). The third use of the term is as "good governance"; I shall have something a little more substantial to say about this later, so will leave further exegesis until then.

For the purposes of this chapter I focus in particular on two aspects of the changes in the nature, role, and place of the state that are occurring simultaneously. The first is that the state's role in the governance of education has changed from a role where the state did it all to a situation where the state has become the coordinator of coordination. The second is that we no longer view the national level as the exclusive scale at which the governance of education takes place. That is to say, the ways that education systems are coordinated in order to deliver, among other things, "solutions" to the core problems have changed considerably; at the same time, those things take place in the context of a qualitatively changed relationship between nation-states and the global order. Today, no nation-states are isolated or insulated from the effects of economic, and indeed, political globalization. In this process, the state has been not so much replaced or removed, in the sense of its subsumption under a different set of institutions, but rather re-placed, or displaced, in the sense that it no longer occupies the same space that it did in its postwar heyday. It is not so much a-topic, as ectopic; not so much without a place as out of place.

These changes have been brought about in a number of ways as states' responses to globalization (and it is crucial to note that states themselves have been among the most active agents of globalization). It will be useful to consider the relationships between states and globalization as falling, analytically, into three categories, those of direct, (specific, intended, and predictable), indirect (unspecific, intended, and predictable) and collateral (unspecific, unintended, but predictable) effects.

As an aside, I use the term *effects* with some caution, since it might easily be taken as meaning an exclusively top-down or unidirectional relationship between globalization and nation-states. This is not at all the intent. As I have just suggested, states (certainly Western states) themselves are among the strongest agents of globalization, and might be seen as willing and witting participants or partners in the relationship with the other agents of globalization (especially other states with whom they enter into the kinds of agreements that propel it), rather than as more or less helpless victims. This is clear, I hope, in the definitions of the three categories. The reason for retaining the term *effects* is that this is how they tend to be experienced and represented at national state level, and so long as the major caveats just outlined are respected, it seems preferable to use the term rather than becoming involved in spelling out the complicated arguments that lie behind them on each occasion that they are discussed.

Since my main focus here is with regard to the second stance, indirect effects of globalization on education governance, I will first briefly mention the first and third categories.

First definition: The best examples of direct effects are those that would make education itself a commodity to be traded on the global market. This process, and its possible consequences, is most evident in the discussions around the treatment of education under the GATS [See Robertson, Bonal, and Dale (2003) and the special issue (vol. 1, no. 3, 2004) of *Globalization, Societies, and Education*].

Third definition: By collateral effects I mean such developments as migration, child labor, and household competition.

INDIRECT EFFECTS EXPLORED

The indirect effects that I want to mention, none of which are aimed specifically at education but all of which have profound and predictable consequences for national education systems, are generated by three interlinked sources.

Source One

The first of these is what has been called the "constitutionalization of the neoliberal" (Gill 1995). What this means is that neoliberalism, the ideological driving force of globalization and that sees the expansion of free trade and the elimination of all barriers to it as crucial, has a rather different conception of the state from that of classical liberalism, which essentially sought always to minimize that role. Neoliberals share that purpose, but see it as advancing more rapidly by making the state a partner rather than an obstacle to their achievement. Thus, we see the enactment of "state-reducing" strategies by states themselves, on the grounds, for instance, that the private sector is more efficient, or that there are limits to the amount of tax-supported, electorally acceptable intervention. The apogee of neoliberalism was probably the Washington Consensus, a set of precepts distilled from the approaches of the major international financial institutions (IMF, World Bank, and others) about what was appropriate action for states to take in respect of the economy. These included:

- Fiscal discipline
- Redirection of public expenditure
- Tax reform
- Interest rate liberalization
- A competitive exchange rate
- Trade liberalization

- Privatization
- Deregulation
- Secure property rights
  (see Williamson 2000)

When the Washington Consensus appeared to not be delivering what was intended, possibly because of its harshness, the World Bank came up with an alternative approach, this time based on *good governance* (the title indicates the degree to which reform of the state was seen as central). This was linked with an "ideology of statehood that reigned virtually unchallenged after the failure of the USSR . . . based on the principles of multi-party democracy, respect for human rights, and 'good governance,' together with a view of the state as the essential manager of a regulated market economy, with responsibility notably for the legal order, the currency and infrastructure, and the provision of basic social services" (Clapham 2002, 789).

Good governance is a normative as well as /rather than an analytic concept. It promoted the form of *best practice* whose aims are fundamentally to boost global investor confidence by:

- Placing market regulatory institutions beyond the reach of governments
- Creating independent regulatory institutions
- Creating a set of institutions to structural adjustment programs
- Shifting national governments from provision to regulation
  (adapted from Jayasuriya, [1999])

More recently, the Harvard economist Dani Rodrik (2001) has put forward the features of what he calls the "augmented" Washington Consensus, which pursues essentially the same purposes through slightly different means. These are:

- Corporate governance
- Anti-corruption
- Flexible labor markets
- WTO agreements
- Financial codes and standards
- "Prudent" capital-account openings
- Independent central banks/inflation targeting
- Social safety nets
- Targeted poverty reduction

Two other examples of the constitutionalization of the neoliberals are the European Monetary System (Euro and Broad Economic Policy Guidelines) and, of particular significance for this discussion, the (generic) New Public Management, which emerged as a key means of implementing the neoliberal agenda in the area of governance.

Source Two

The second source of indirect effect generators is a range of collective responses made by nation-states voluntarily ceding elements of their autonomy or sovereignty to supranational bodies in order better to protect their own interests than would be possible for them individually. Putting it simply, these responses aimed to continue to expand free trade—but in ways that would prevent it from destroying itself while delivering its benefits to the members of the collective. One model of such collectives includes major international organizations such as the OECD and the G8/9, whose membership comprises the richest countries of the world and whose aim is to ensure that they continue to benefit from the development of the world economy (albeit that they argue that this can be achieved not only not to the detriment of, but also on the basis of the increased prosperity of, the poorer countries of the world). Regional organizations like the EU, NAFTA, and APEC are another, varying set of examples, developed on the basis of the recognition that individual states did not have the means to "shape" or "resist" the forces of globalization and that they would be better able to do so collectively. The regional organizations may be seen as clubs operating in the collective interest of their members, but requiring those members to adhere to the collective rules and procedures. (The degree to which they are literally rule-bound varies, with APEC relying on consensus and concerted multilateralism rather than any formal rules.) Their policies seek to simultaneously drive forward and realize the major benefits of the development of free trade, but in ways that would enable them both to protect themselves from its worst implications. The developments at Cancun (September 12–14, 2003, a forum in which the EU as an organization speaks on behalf of all its members) have demonstrated this rather clearly.

Source Three

The third source is the "globalization of production," which has two very significant indirect effects on education systems. First, the changing global division of labor means that national education systems are called on to respond to different patterns of demand for the human capital it is thought that they are able to supply. Second, the scalar shift of economic activity away from the national scale entails a shift in scale of the *institutional embedding* (mode of regulation), in which education plays a key part, and on which continuing economic development rests.

The first of these sets of indirect effects, the neoliberal project, involves changes in the patterns of governance of education systems; the second, the collectivizing of risk and sharing benefits of globalization, involves changes in the scale of that governance; and the third, the globalization of production, involves changes in both simultaneously.

GOVERNANCE AND SCALE

The critical point when the need for a quite new account of the relationship between the state and education became evident came with the discussions of the so-called privatization of education that ran through the 1980s and gathered force during the early 1990s, especially in Anglophone countries. While very much open to the idea that schools were being privatized, I could see very little evidence of it. The quantity of private schools did not seem to be rising dramatically, there was no significantly greater private financing of compulsory schooling, and there was little evidence of encouragement or incentives to schools to become commercial operations. However, some very significant changes were taking place that had to be addressed. The conclusion I drew was one that came readily to mind in the New Zealand of the early 1990s. The changes were not the result of a shift in responsibility from one institution to another—the state to the market or the community—but essentially a change in the role and operation of the state, brought about by close and explicit attachment to the neoliberal project. In particular, I became attracted to the idea of governance as a possible way of understanding these changes. In "The State and the Governance of Education" (Dale 1997), I argued that if we divided up the operation of education systems into its distinct component parts, which I took to be funding, provision, and regulation (later, ownership was added), and looked to see how and by whom they were carried out, we would find that they certainly need not be, and historically had not been, all carried out by the state. So, I suggested the possibility of a division of labor between the state and the market and community (the subsequent addition of "household" reflected the growing contribution of paying private fees even within state education, as well as to make the model more robust cross-nationally). This division might be involved in at least some elements of the operation of education systems. The overall process I referred to as the Governance of Education. It was graphically reflected in a 3x3 matrix (F/P/RxS/M/C) that I saw as a key to understanding not only changes in the relationship between state and education, but also the coordination of education, which could be achieved through potentially any combination of activities and institutions. That led, paradoxically, to an intensified focus on the state, since it was apparent that what lay behind the claims of privatization were, in the great majority of cases, major changes in the role and activities of the state, very broadly in the direction of "steering." So rather than doing everything itself, the state now determined what body would do it. That is to say, the state took on the role of *coordinator of coordination*.

It is also important and helpful to note that it is not that there was no "governance" before 1989 or whenever—but that we were able to take for granted the forms that it took, forms that became so familiar to us that we did not recognize what lay beneath and behind them. To put it another way, one of the benefits to be gained from looking closely at governance is that it reveals the degree to which we have tended to, in a sense, fetishize the postwar social democratic state and to see departures from it as pathological rather than trying to theorize them. One prominent argument, with which I have considerable sympathy, is that governance should not be associated with the death of the state. It insists that the state is still of central relevance, but that its forms and methods have changed. Another, which I also find persuasive, is that states have lost power to supranational organizations, and that that is where governance is to be found. And the third, which also has persuasive elements, sees governance as a bottom-up, grassroots response to changes in the nature of rule that is fed by social capital and civil society. The problem with these approaches is that they all, to some degree, adopt a zero-sum assumption of the scope of globalization in their analyses. That is, they seem to suggest that if there is evidence of governance at one scalar level, there will not be any at other levels; while they recognize the nature of the changes taking place, they tend to seek to confine them to a particular level of rule or government. This may be something of an exaggeration, but it does indicate one vital point to be made, that in a globalizing era, different forms of governance can be expected at all emerging levels of the polity. The question then becomes, as it essentially always should have been, had it not been occluded by the assumptions of social democracy, what forms of governance are in place where and why—and putting the question in this form enables us to recognize, respond, and seek to identify the nature and consequences of different national traditions and trajectories. So, the recognition the state had never done it all— and that at least the great majority of the activities of governing were not dependent on the state doing them—led to the view that governance, construed as the coordination of coordination, was the appropriate concept with which to address issues of government; in a sense, the state moved from being *explanans* to *explanadum*.

A further key development of the governance idea came through an attempt to investigate these ideas empirically. This was achieved through a grant (awarded jointly to Susan Robertson) from the Marsden Fund of the Royal Society of New Zealand to look at the competitive-contractual state in four similarly-sized English-speaking regions with similarly based but divergently developed education systems—Alberta (Canada), New Zealand, Scotland, and Singapore. The most significant element of this research for current purposes concerned the four systems' relationship to regional organizations (APEC, EU, and NAFTA). These turned out to be as varied as had been expected, though it seemed that the variation was around a much more common agenda. It also made it necessary, however, to add a third dimension to the governance diagram, to take account of the different scales at which the activities of education systems might be funded, regulated, owned, and provided (see Dale and Robertson 2003). Studies of the governance of education would now need to take into account other scales than the national. Of the regional organizations we studied, the most significant by far turned out to be the EU, largely because the research into its relationship with national education systems, which existing work had (quite rightly) suggested was minimal, took place in 2000, the year of the EU Lisbon Summit. This turned out to be a major watershed, not only in the relationship between Europe and national education systems, but in the future direction and organization of the EU itself (see Dale 2003a, 2003b; Dale and Robertson 2003).

This made it clear that the governance of education is now a *pluri-scalar* matter (see figure 3.1). We refer to *pluri-scalar governance* (a) because it takes place at potentially several different scales, rather than exclusively at the level of the nation-state; (b) because it is not *international*, with its implications of multiple locations (typically nation-states) on the same scale. It is governance because its assumptions are wider than the state-bureaucratic assumptions that have often characterized comparative education. What we are now witnessing is (a) a shift away from the state taking direct responsibility for all the activities of rule itself, and to the state determining who will take responsibility for them, and (b) the need for the national scale combinations of activities and institutions of governance to be augmented by the recognition that potentially any or all of these activities might also be governed at a different *scale*. And this approach is particularly helpful when we apply it to both the functional and the scalar division of the labor of educational governance—that is, that activities of governance may be fragmented across scales rather than distributed as "wholes." There is a clear need to identify and explicate the nature and effects of the mechanisms through which education systems and practices that take place at, are decided at, affect, are integrated into, and cohere with different scales, are brought into relationship with each other.

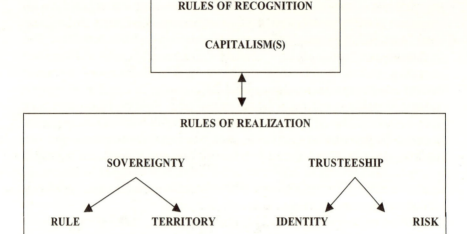

Figure 3.1. Global Capitalism and the Operation of the Nation-State

What we understand by the scalar division of the labor of educational governance is represented in figure 3.1, which is intended to indicate the complexity of what is involved in governance and to show the possibility that all the combinations of activities and actors might be performed at any of the levels and not just on the national stage. However, that leaves wide open the question of the ways in which those combinations might be executed and with what effects. We have attempted (with a view to making them comparable) a fairly rudimentary mapping of some of these possibilities elsewhere, but for the purpose of this presentation we wish to concentrate on the dimension of power in operation.

UNDERSTANDING GOVERNANCE

Understanding governance entails stepping back a little to consider the changing nature of the nation-state and its relationships with *globalization* on the one hand and *education* on the other. The basic argument in respect of the nation-state is that it has certainly changed, but that those changes have been uneven and complex rather than the simple erosion of sovereignty or autonomy. The argument then does not see a zero-sum relationship between state and globalization, but rather goes back to consider the historical development of the Westphalian state—and in particular its configuration in the *trente glo-*

rieuses. This has come to be taken as a kind of normative benchmark of what the state can and should be doing, with departures from it seen as pathological and morally bankrupt betrayals, rather than as developed responses to changing external circumstances.

It will be useful to go back to some basic principles.

The modern conception of the nation-state grew around three key nodes: its *sovereignty*; its *trusteeship*; and its *relationship to capitalism*, in all of which state education systems are fundamentally involved. It is also useful to spell out the relationship between these three nodes. This relationship is best captured by Bernstein's conception of the rules of recognition and realization. He distinguishes them as follows:

> Recognition rules create the means of distinguishing between and so recognizing the speciality that constitutes a context, and realization rules regulate the creation and production of specialized relationships internal to that context (Bernstein 1981, 328–29).

These sets of rules may also be seen to underpin the distribution of power and the principles of control. One example Bernstein gave of the distinction concerned the clothing to be worn at a wedding and a funeral. We know that certain things are not worn on such occasions (rule of regulation), but within those categories there is a great deal of scope for personal choice (rule of recognition).

In this case, I want to suggest that *capitalism* sets the rules of *recognition* — which may and do vary considerably and importantly, but which contain a common and irreducible core — and that *sovereignty and trusteeship* are (distinct) sets of rules of *realization*. Another way of seeing the operations of the rules of recognition, which is especially useful in the case of a system like capitalism — that has demonstrated the ability to live easily with a number of different sets of rules of recognition and realization — is that they should be seen as *exclusive* rather than inclusive, *proscriptive* rather than prescriptive. It should, of course, be noted that (a) the rules of recognition vary greatly for different sectors of capital; (b) there are intrinsic and crucial points of contradiction in the relationship between the two sets of rules; and (c) the relationship between the two sets of rules is by no means constant (Keynes vs. Schumpeter, for example; see Jessop 1999).

Second, I want to suggest that the collective consequence of the kinds of effects of globalization on national states that I have just described has been a "decoupling" of what were tightly bound elements of both sovereignty and trusteeship, though the forms and mechanisms were different in the two cases. Roughly, sovereignty was effected from above (direct/indirect), and trusteeship from below (indirect/collateral damage). In the case of sovereignty there have been relevant recent critiques of the concept, suggesting that on the one hand it is not to be taken as an absolute concept (Jayasuriya 1999; 2001) and on the other that "sovereignty is not about state control but state authority" (Thomson 1995, 216). However, the main point I wish to make here is that, albeit implicitly, ideas of *rule* and *territory* were unproblematically taken as very highly, even necessarily, mutually imbricated in sovereignty, to the point where the possibility of any separation between them tended to become lost; sovereignty meant exclusive rule over a territory. That is, rule and territory as elements of sovereignty have always been there but were too obvious to be noticed. Under current conditions, however, the separation of governance and scale is increasingly evident. In the case of trusteeship, the "common community of fate," based on common sacrifice and cohesion, that the state held in trust, is becoming bifurcated into its affirmation and protection, identity and risk elements.

RULES OF THE GAME

In the context of this chapter it is important to note the relationship between rule and governance. Governance as the coordination of coordination of the activities of a sector is but one, albeit quite crucial, element of what is involved in ruling. One useful way of conceiving of the relationship between them may be inferred from comments made by Boyer and Dehove (2001). They suggest that the Cabinet (or Conseil d'Etat) in modern states has three main responsibilities or tasks with respect to *ruling*. First, it determines the norms through which the agenda of government is established. Second, it frames the considerations of the legislature, taking into account the relevant techniques and interests, and the national preference, so that it expresses the ideas of those making up the political majority. Third, it selects the means of engagement and coordinates them; it chooses when to put them into practice and how they will be justified, and how to make them acceptable to public opinion.

The argument here is that governance as the coordination of coordination is present in all these tasks. In this sense, it works according to Lukes' third dimension of power, in setting the rules of the game. But if we take governance as the coordination of coordination, we are left with something of a problem over the issue of regulation. In the original formulation of the governance argument, I suggested that all that was necessary for states to retain control of education systems, for education systems to remain state systems, was that the state retained control of regulation. Essentially, regulation was seen as the means through which the coordination of coordination could be implemented. However, it is necessary for a number of reasons to revisit that assumption.

The first reason is that empirically it has become clear, certainly in the case of the United Kingdom, that states have not retained control of education regulation. The outcomes of the reforms to the governance of education of the later 1990s, that saw partnership between the state and other bodies and the devolution of some aspects of the governance of education to local bodies or individual schools, have demonstrated that the state has not been able to retain complete control over regulation. The best examples here are probably the experience of public-private partnerships and of the contracting out to private firms the educational administration in some local authorities; in none of these cases has the state been able to retain or impose regulation effectively.

Theoretically, too, we might expect a change in the nature and meaning of regulation. It is clear that the form of regulation under the constitutionalization of the neoliberal has changed fundamentally. We have become accustomed to seeing this summed as a shift from ex ante to ex post, from regulation of and through inputs to regulation of and through outputs. However, there may be more at issue here in the education area, where we may be seeing what could be an equally, if not more, significant change, the put down to the rescaling of educational governance. This is the shift from the measurement/determination of *outputs* to the measurement/determination of *outcomes*, that is, the measurement of achievement of aims as well as, or rather than, the achievement of objectives. In education we might take the New Zealand example as instructive. There, the *minister* is responsible for setting outcomes she or he wants to achieve through the work of the education system, and the *ministry* is responsible for transforming these into a set of outputs for schools, on the basis of which they will be assessed. We can see evidence of this in the supranational agendas for education and the Knowledge Economy and Lifelong Learning, for instance, while the development of PISA, based on competences rather than certificates, may be a concrete example.

If sovereignty must be reassessed, and regulation is the key means through which sovereignty is expressed and maintained, then we should expect changes in the form and status of regulation. The most effective way of capturing these changes may be as a shift from *control* to *authority*. The question then becomes the degree to which nonstate involvement in regulation is possible without undermining the state's authority, and its responsibility for the prosperity, well-being, and security of its citizens. This is all the more an issue when we take into account the possible rescaling of responsibility for educational governance. We might compare the issue of currency here: just as the argument for the ceding of national currencies and the embrace of a supranational currency is that it is justified by the positive trade-offs—the national state will be better able to serve its citizens by ceding some areas of national sovereignty to supranational bodies, or accepting supranational regulation in areas where it previously held exclusive competence—so the argument for rescaling some elements of the governance of education must be that it will enable better outcomes for the national population than retaining national control. It is crucial to reemphasize here that this is not a zero-sum game; indeed, it seems likely that the partial rescaling the regulation of elements of national education systems might well exacerbate the contradictions between the core problems and between them and the national security/identity problem.

So, we might say that here globalization does not replace, but reduces (though in some cases it might also extend), reallocates, refocuses, and rescales the regulatory role of the state—but it does not wholly surrender that role, as it retains in some cases the role of funder, provider, and owner. How far and in what areas this may occur becomes a matter both for empirical investigation and for theoretical reflection about the state as explanandum.

In terms of governance then, we might argue that the *ectopic* state (and of course, as will be evident by now is that the ectopic conception itself rests on a conception of a proper place for the state) is not able to *control* how governance as the coordination of coordination is achieved but that it retains both *authority* to do so and the *responsibility* for it. The authority is based in the state's continuing ability to set the rules of the game (as set out, for instance, by Boyer and Dehove). The state remains the coordinator and regulator of last resort (for instance, where self-regulation fails—such as in the New Zealand education industry; see Lewis 2005); it continues to take responsibility for the failure of coordination or the abuse of regulation. (A prime example here is the complete failure of the forced replacement of the public body running education in the London Borough of Southwark by a private firm, which turned out to be "an unmitigated disaster," with the private firm pulling out of its five-year contract two years early, leaving "a trail of educational and financial misery"; see Toolis 2003.)

CONCLUSION

I want to make four points in conclusion to this chapter.

1. The analysis of governance requires an analysis of changes to the state itself; it indicates that the state has to be much more explanandum than explanans. On this basis, we can see that many of the functions taken to be intrinsically and necessarily *state* functions are not necessarily so. It is also essential to revisit the notion of state control. It may not be necessary—or possible—for the state to control all the areas over which it exercises authority and responsibility for it to retain its importance. As coordinator of coordination, the state sets the rules of the political economic game. As regulator of last resort, the state is still the only body expected to and capable of address-

ing the three core problems of accumulation, order, and legitimation, and of resolving or at least seeking to resolve the contradictions within and between them.

2. It is important to recognize that governance is not a neutral activity. The rules of the game not only shape what is possible for whom and how, but they are always what Jessop calls "strategically selective"; they favor some interests over others. This is clear in what we have been discussing in the way that neoliberalism is deliberately aimed at advancing some interest at the expense of others—and it is especially important as we move toward greater supranational involvement in the governance of education.

3. Throughout the past decade, and seemingly likely to continue, the reform of governance has been the key means of reforming education. In an era that seems to be characterized by an ambition to transform rather than incrementally improve education systems and practices, the reform of governance is the necessary first step, whether it involves changes to the control of pedagogy or revisions of conceptions of educational time and space. This is especially evident in the area of ICT (Information and Communication Technology), but is by no means confined to it.

4. Finally, we may expect some changes in the functional, scalar, and sectoral division of the labor of educational governance, involving a significant, if not extensive, reallocation of activities, institutions, individuals, and outcomes in education.

BIBLIOGRAPHY

Boyer, Robert, and Mario Dehove (2001). "Theories de l'Integration Europeenne: Entre Gouvernace et Gouvernement," *La lettre de la regulation* 38, 1–4.

Clapham, Christopher (2002). "The Challenge to the State in a Globalised World," *Development and Change* 33, no. 5, 775–95.

Dale, Roger (1989). *The State and Education Policy*. Buckingham, UK: Open University Press.

Dale, Roger (1992). "Recovering from a Pyrrhic Victory? Quality, Relevance and Impact in the Sociology of Education." In *Voicing Concerns: Sociological Perspectives on Contemporary Educational Reforms*, ed. M. Arnot and L. Barton. Wallingford, UK: Triangle Books.

Dale, Roger (1997). "The State and the Governance of Education: An Analysis of the Restructuring of the State–Education Relationship." In *Education: Culture, Economy and Society*, A. H. Halsey, H. Lauder, P. Brown. and A. S. Wells. Oxford, UK: Oxford University Press, 273–82.

Dale, Roger (2003a). The Lisbon Declaration, the Reconceptualization of Governance, and the Reconfiguration of European Educational Space. Paper presented to RAPPE Seminar University of London Institute of Education, March 20.

Dale, Roger (2003b). Globalization, Europeanization, and the "Competitiveness" Agenda: Implications for Education Policy in Europe. Paper presented to GENIE Conference, Nicosia, July 10.

Dale, Roger, and Susan Robertson (2003). "Regional Organisations as Subjects of Globalisation," *Comparative Education Review* 46, no. 1: 10–36.

Fine, Ben (2001). *Social Capital versus Social Theory: Political Economy and Social Science at the Turn of the Millennium.* London: Routledge.

Fukuyama, Francis (1995). *Trust: The Social Virtues and the Creation of Prosperity.* London: Penguin.

Gill, Stephen (1995). "Market Civilization and Global Disciplinary Neoliberalism," *Millennium: Journal of International Studies* 25, no 3: 399–423.

Jessop, Bob (1999). "The Changing Governance of Welfare: Recent Trends in its Primary Functions, Scale, and Modes of Coordination," *Social Policy and Administration* 33, no. 4: 348–59.

Jayasuriya, Kanishka (1999). "Globalization, Law, and the Transformation of Sovereignty: The Emergence of Global Regulatory Governance," *Indiana Journal of Global Legal Studies* 6, no. 2: 425–56.

Jayasuriya, Kanishka (2001). "Globalization, Sovereignty, and the Rule of Law: From Political to Economic Constitutionalism?" *Constellations* 8, no. 4: 442–60.

Lewis, Nicolas (2005). "Code of Practice for the Pastoral Care of International Students: Making a Globalising Industry in New Zealand," *Globalisation, Societies and Education* 3, no. 1: 5–47.

Putnam, R. D., ed. (2002). *Democracies in Flux: The Evolution of Social Capital in Contemporary Society.* New York: Oxford University Press.

Robertson, Susan, Xavier Bonal, and Roger Dale (2003). "GATS and Education," *Comparative Education Review* 46, no. 4: 472–96.

Rodrik, Dani. (2001). *The Global Governance of Trade as if Development Really Mattered.* New York: UNDP.

Rosenau, J., and E.-O. Cziempel (1992). *Governance without Government: Order and Change in World Politics.* Cambridge, UK: Cambridge University Press.

Thomson, Janice E. (1995). "State Sovereignty in International Relations: Bridging the Gap betweeen Theory and Empirical Research," *International Studies Quarterly* 39, 213–33.

Toolis, Kevin (2003). "Will They Ever Learn?" *Guardian*, November 22.

Williamson, John (2000). "What Should the World Bank Think about the Washington Consensus?" *World Bank Research Observer* 15, no. 2, 251–64.

4

Human Rights and Citizenship

The Emergence of Human Rights Education

David F. Suarez and Francisco O. Ramirez

A recurring theme in the sociology of education is that schooling produces citizenship or a sense of membership in the nation-state. Much of the literature on civic education explores this theme, either lamenting school failures in this arena or fearing that hyper-successful schools will create massive conformity. Different though these perspectives are, they share the premise that schooling is designed to produce national citizens, with the national heritage and the nation-state as the crucial and bounded referential standards. This premise is challenged by the development of the human rights movement and its more recent human rights education focus. Human rights awareness has emerged as an influential discourse and this discourse is changing from a solely legal to a broader human rights education focus. Civic education, once the central curricular area for teaching national citizenship, now teaches global citizenship and incorporates a rights discourse that extends beyond national borders.

Human rights education (HRE) increasingly is a major theme in educational systems around the world. The topic is advanced in world organizations, professional associations, and international advocacy groups. Moreover, human rights education principles have penetrated curricular plans, policies, and practices in many national societies. National history and civics courses in varying degrees adapt to the HRE revolution. The rise and spread of human rights education reflects broad processes of cultural globalization over recent decades. Cultural globalization involves the worldwide spread of models or blueprints of progress and the networks of organizations and experts that transmit these logics of appropriateness to nation-states and other collectivities. The changing state of the world and of national linkages to world society account for the rise in human rights education organization and discourse—and we expect that as cultural globalization continues, human rights concepts will become more prevalent in national curricula.[1]

Human rights education is a developing field and a curricular movement that the United Nations defined as "training, dissemination, and information efforts aimed at the building of a universal culture of human rights through the imparting of knowledge and skills and the [molding] of attitudes" (United Nations 1998, 3). Human rights education began with the work of nongovernmental organizations (NGOs) in informal education and popular education but, in recent decades, HRE has become much more prevalent in a variety of settings throughout the world. Human rights education is developing in formal education systems for students at different levels (primary, secondary, and tertiary) and is becoming more common in training for diverse professional groups (teachers, lawyers, police officers, and psychologists). Moreover, a variety of organizations, groups, and actors have become involved in the movement, including intergovernmental organizations (IGOs), nongovernmental organizations (NGOs), foundations, religious organizations, professional organizations, and academic organizations. By 1995, human rights education had gained enough momentum that the United Nations proclaimed that year to be the beginning of the United Nations Decade for Human Rights Education (1995–2004).

Cultural globalization has produced two dramatic worldwide changes that fuel this movement for human rights education. One is the human rights movement itself and the degree to which this brings about a shift in perspective from the individual as a citizen and a member of the nation to the person as a human member of world society. A second shift is the enormous expansion of education and its diffuse empowerment of individual persons. This expansion in the salience and prevalence of HRE thus has its roots in the broader human rights movement and in the empowerment of the individual in the modern world polity. This chapter charts the history and expansion of human rights education at the world level and relates these developments to the human rights movement and the empowerment of individuals through education. We begin by providing a brief description of the human rights movement and then focus on the emergence and development of human rights education. We conclude by relating human rights education to civic education and changing notions of citizenship.

THE EXPANSION OF HUMAN RIGHTS

Most international developments in the modern human rights movement began to take place after World War I. Before World War I, there were some international campaigns such as the effort to abolish slavery, but for the most part these campaigns involved just a few dedicated nongovernmental organizations (Keck and Sikkink 1998; Lauren 2000). Nations were not particularly concerned with human rights violations within the borders of foreign nations, and the Convention of the League of Nations after World War I contained no mention of human rights. After World War II, however, the panorama changed substantially.

The horrors of the Holocaust during World War II had a major impact on the development of the human rights movement. Although countries continued to wave the banner of sovereignty, the United Nations was formed in 1945 and the Universal Declaration of Human Rights was set forth in 1948. For the first time, human rights became a global issue and represented a worldwide model for appropriate state behavior. Particular ideas have more strength than others and domestic conditions often distort and translate international scripts, but human rights discourse has had a pervasive influence. With the growing legitimacy of human rights, states and other actors have started to pay attention to issues involving the protection of human rights. After the creation of the Universal Declaration of Human Rights it became possible to argue that "what started as a Western cultural account is now universal, and there is evidence of its growing intensification" (Ramirez 1987, 327). Since World War II the number of human rights organizations has expanded dramatically (Tiberghien 1997; Wiseberg and Scoble 1981). Based on data from the Human Rights Internet and the Union of International Associations, figure 4.1 captures the number of human rights organizations that were founded on a yearly basis between 1839 and 1995. As the figure shows, the formation of human rights organizations before World War II was fairly constant but quite low in terms of "foundings" per year. The figure also demonstrates that there was a noticeable increase in the formation of human rights organizations just after World War II and following the creation of the United Nations. The most interesting aspect of the figure, however, is the period after the 1960s. In every year between 1970 and the mid-1990s, the number of organizations founded exceeded the number of organizations founded in any previous year.

Developments in intergovernmental organizations and in foundations paralleled the developments in NGOs. Before the creation of the Universal Declaration of Human Rights there were no intergovernmental organizations focused on human rights but, by 1990, human rights was emphasized in twenty-seven organizations (Keck and Sikkink 1998). Funding for foundations followed a similar pattern. In the early 1970s "the big U.S. foundations hardly ever funded international human rights work. From 1977 to 1987, however, such grant making grew dramatically, both in numbers of grants and

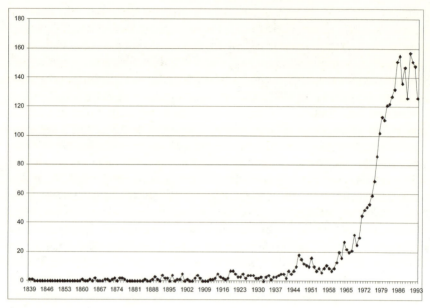

Figure 4.1.

in their total dollar amount" (Keck and Sikkink 1998, 98). In every respect, then, interest in human rights increased dramatically—in recent decades foundations began to increase funding to human rights, the number of NGOs involved in the movement increased, and the number of IGOs involved in human rights also increased. These developments in human rights paralleled many changes taking place in education.

EDUCATION AND HUMAN RIGHTS EDUCATION

Besides being an era of growth in the human rights movement, the post–World War II era also was a time of enormous educational growth. Poor countries, which had almost no education in 1950, had nearly universal primary enrollments (of admittedly varying quality) and greatly expanded secondary enrollments by the end of the century (see Meyer et al. 1992 and 1977, for cross-national analyses of primary enrollment growth). University-level education occurs now in every country and many less-developed countries today show tertiary enrollment rates greater than those found in Britain, France, or Germany in 1960 (Schofer and Meyer 2005). Beyond general enrollment growth, expanded education has involved an increase in (a) the range of groups and interests identified within education, such as ethnic, regional, or gender groups, (b) the range of topics covered in national education and school curricula, and (c) the range of national and individual goals education is expected to serve. Virtually every domain of social life is now included in the school system; students learn not only some skills and norms to prepare them for future occupational and political roles but also identities in terms of ethnicity and gender and other collective subnational bases.

These trends in the growth and complexity of both education and the human rights movement continued, and beginning in the late 1970s a variety of organizations began to link the world of human rights and the world of education. Early work in the human rights movement involved promoting human rights declarations and instruments (Wiseberg and Scoble 1981). Because of the importance of promoting these declarations and instruments, during the first few decades of the human rights movement there was little work in human rights education in formal school settings and almost all human rights education involved legal training. Much of the "action" in human rights was taking place either at a very grassroots level or at the international level in IGOs like the United Nations. The emphasis was legal because nations were signing documents that were supposed to become international laws. As one human rights educator noted, in the 1970s:

> Much of what was defined as human rights education was shaped principally by lawyers. . . . Not surprisingly, on a practical or methodological level, this often led to a focus on the law and a formal discussion of rights as the entry point to human rights education (Miller 2002).

As time passed, however, the legal emphasis began to change and human rights educators began to see the relevance of human rights for formal education systems. This does not imply that the legal aspects of HRE disappeared or became less relevant, but it does suggest that HRE underwent an important transformation. Researchers and practitioners began to recognize that to promote human rights required educational activity, not merely legal training (Martin et al. 1997; Claude 1997). These changes are reflected in the growing salience of human rights education in nations, in intergovernmental organizations, and in nongovernmental organizations.

Human Rights Education in Intergovernmental Organizations

Although it is possible to point to the creation of the United Nations as the beginning of human rights education, very few efforts were made to teach human rights until more recent decades. The United Nations Charter endorsed efforts at "promoting and encouraging respect for human rights and fundamental freedoms" (United Nations 1945) and the Preamble of the Universal

Table 4.1.   Major International and Regional Events in the History of Human Rights Education

Year	Event
1945	United Nations Established
1948	Universal Declaration of Human Rights
1952	International Seminar on Teaching About Human Rights (Netherlands)
1953	UNESCO Associated Schools Project Established
1974	UNESCO Recommendation on Human Rights Education
1978	UNESCO Prize for Human Rights Education Established
1978	First International Congress on the Teaching of Human Rights (Austria)
1978	Council of Europe Resolution (78) 41 on the Teaching of Human Rights
1979	Asia-Pacific Meeting of Experts in Education for Peace and Human Rights
1981	African Charter on Human and Peoples' Rights (Banjul)
1982	Meeting of Experts in Human Rights Teaching (Strasbourg)
1983	International Conference on Human Rights and Fundamental Freedoms (Paris)
1984	First Latin American Conference on Human Rights Education (Venezuela)
1985	Council of Europe Recommendation R (85) 7 on Teaching about Human Rights in Schools
1987	International Congress on Human Rights Teaching, Information, and Documentation (Malta)
1988	Additional Protocol to the American Convention on Human Rights (Protocol of San Salvador)
1989	First Meeting of Directors of Human Rights Research and Training Institutes
1992	International Meeting on Human Rights Education (Czech Rep.)
1993	International Congress on Education for Human Rights and Democracy (Canada)
1993	World Conference on Human Rights (Austria)
1994	UNESCO Academic Chair in Human Rights Education Created
1995	United Nations Decade for Human Rights Education Established

Source: Branson and Torney-Purta (1982); Tiberghien (1997), Suarez (2004b)

Declaration for Human Rights stated that nations should "strive by teaching and education to promote respect for these rights and freedoms" (United Nations 1948).

Nevertheless, work in HRE evolved incrementally and unevenly. The United Nations Educational, Scientific, and Cultural Organization (UNESCO) has always been the biggest proponent of human rights education at the IGO level, and UNESCO made a first attempt with the creation of the Associated Schools Project in 1953. The Associated Schools Project supported experimental schools in different regions of the world in order to promote the Universal Declaration of Human Rights and to promote the activities of the United Nations (UNESCO 2003b). Teaching human rights was thus just one of many goals of the program. This project followed the first international seminar on teaching human rights (1952) and the program still exists today. While the program continues to grow and serve more schools in more countries, it is not clear how much human rights awareness was actually taught in these schools in the first few decades of the program.

As mentioned earlier, the human rights movement was still in its early phases in the 1950s, and few countries were willing to allow these UNESCO schools to operate freely within their borders. In the United States, for example, the fear of communism took hold after World War II and in 1951 a "controversy erupted over a locally designed curriculum unit on UNESCO and its teachers' manual, which supposedly promoted 'faceless citizenship in a monstrous world government'" (Zimmerman 2002, 86–87). The United Nations and UNESCO were treated with caution even by the nations that helped to form them, and curriculum units that did nothing more than introduce these organizations were often regarded as suspect or even subversive. It is thus not surprising that UNESCO characterized these initial efforts with Associated Schools as "grassroots" (UNESCO 2003b). Human rights education was still a long way from the mainstream and the Associated Schools Project was just the first step in this direction, but table 4.1 demonstrates the tremendous growth of the program over time.

Other than the Associated Schools Project, UNESCO and all other intergovernmental organizations were virtually silent when it came to human rights education. In fact, as table 4.2 indicates, the topic dropped off the agenda for intergovernmental organizations until the 1970s. In 1974, human rights education reappeared on the scene with the UNESCO Recommendation Concerning Education for International Understanding, Cooperation and Peace and Education Relating to Human Rights and Fundamental Freedoms (UNESCO 1974). Compared to a treaty, this document did not have the power to regulate or mandate specific activities. More than anything else, the Recommendation elaborated on and clarified the UNESCO vision of the curriculum and the social sciences. In all, seventy-six countries signed the

Table 4.2.   UNESCO Associated Schools Program
(Participating Countries and Number of Schools)

Country	1953		1971		2003	
Africa	0	(0)	10	(71)	44	(1666)
Arab States	0	(0)	4	(34)	17	(474)
Asia & Pacific	2	(5)	13	(330)	38	(1286)
Europe & North America	10	(25)	27	(406)	45	(2250)
Latin America & Caribbean	3	(3)	9	(55)	30	(1668)

Sources: UNESCO (1954, 1971, 2002)

document (Buergenthal and Torney 1976), indicating at least a symbolic consensus around the social scientific topics that the international community felt should be included in the curriculum.

Interestingly, although the Recommendation reflects what many consider Western ideas and Western development models, only five countries opposed the Recommendation and all of them were highly developed Western countries (United States, France, Germany, Australia, and Canada). Many developed countries did sign the document, but the active opposition by some of the major world powers demonstrates that the Recommendation was not simply a document prepared by countries in the West for other countries in the world. The United States and England in particular were uncomfortable with the "leftist" turn in the United Nations and were cautious about supporting anything affiliated with it. In fact, the United States and England withdrew from UNESCO in 1984. Both of these countries neglected their commitments to UNESCO for well over a decade before rejoining the organization (Great Britain in 1999 and the United States in 2002).

In spite of the political differences between member countries, the UN-ESCO Recommendation was significant because it was the first educational document to directly emphasize the need to both foster respect for human rights and promote knowledge of the international instruments protecting human rights (Branson and Torney-Purta 1982; Torney-Purta 1987). The United Nations Charter and the Universal Declaration for Human Rights vaguely mentioned the importance of teaching human rights, and the Associated Schools Program made important efforts to teach human rights at the grassroots level, but the Recommendation in 1974 was the first instance where teaching human rights in formal education had a prominent position in an international document.

Even though it did not have the support of some of the most powerful nations in the world, UNESCO sponsored and participated in several human rights education meetings in the years following the Recommendation in 1974. In particular, UNESCO created a human rights education prize, it created university chairs in human rights education, and it sponsored a number of conferences dedicated to human rights education. Besides drawing greater attention to HRE, some of the conferences served to clarify the aims of the Recommendation and human rights education in general. At the International Congress on the Teaching of Human Rights in 1978, participants created a document giving guidelines for HRE. This document emphasized that

> Human rights education and teaching must aim at: (i) Fostering the attitudes of tolerance, respect and solidarity inherent in human rights; (ii) Providing knowledge about human rights, in both their national and international dimensions, and the institutions established for their implementation; (iii) Developing the in-

dividual's awareness of the ways and means by which human rights can be translated into social and political reality at both the national and international levels (Torney-Purta 1984, 59–60).

The UNESCO Recommendation and subsequent international conferences represent *global* developments in human rights education, but many of the major regional cultural organizations have also independently passed legislation in support of HRE. For Europe, the Council of Europe passed a resolution in 1978 on teaching human rights to educators and then passed a recommendation in 1985 on teaching HRE in school. In Africa, the Organization of African Unity created the African Charter on Human and Peoples' Rights (Banjul) in 1981, which mentions the "duty to promote and ensure through teaching, education and publication, the respect of the rights and freedoms contained in the present Charter" (OAU 1981). Finally, in 1988 in Latin America, the Organization of American States produced the Additional Protocol to the American Convention on Human Rights (Protocol of San Salvador), which states that

> The States Parties to this Protocol agree that education should be directed towards the full development of the human personality and human dignity and should strengthen respect for human rights, ideological pluralism, fundamental freedoms, justice and peace (OAS 1988).

Support from intergovernmental organizations does not guarantee the success of human rights education at the national level, but the developments in these organizations clearly indicate increasing interest and global support. Moreover, developments in nongovernmental organizations parallel (and often predate) developments in IGOs.

Human Rights Education and Nongovernmental Organizations

While the work done at the IGO level grants legitimacy and visibility to human rights education, much of the practical work on the ground is carried out by nongovernmental organizations. Besides advocating for the integration of human rights concepts into the school curriculum, these organizations produce textbooks, they train teachers in human rights, and they organize networks of human rights educators.

Figure 4.2 captures the expansion in the number of HRE organizations at the world level. While some organizations were founded before 1970, most of the growth in human rights education organizations comes after the UNESCO Recommendation in 1974. It is important to note that although the Recommendation was a key document in the development of human rights

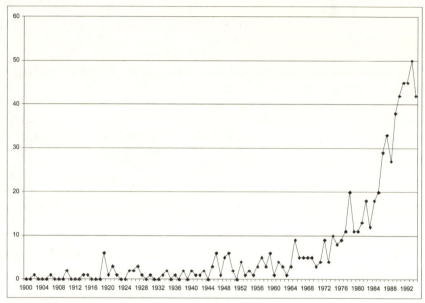

Figure 4.2.

education, it was not necessarily the singular cause for the expansion in human rights education organizations. The human rights movement was cohering during this decade with advocacy efforts in Latin America (Argentina and Chile, in particular)—and both the International Covenant on Civil and Political Rights and the International Covenant on Economic, Social and Cultural Rights went into effect in 1976. The human rights movement was becoming institutionalized enough that formal education was no longer insulated from human rights discourse, and education was also expanding and absorbing a growing variety of populations.

Comparing the growth in human rights organizations to the growth in human rights education organizations demonstrates that education came a bit later. Figure 4.3 suggests that HRE became more of a priority subsequent to the institutionalization of the human rights movement. Amnesty International serves as a good example of this phenomenon. Amnesty International became famous for a singular focus on prisoners of conscience and the protection of civil and political rights. More recently, however, Amnesty International has embraced HRE as a way to prevent future abuses. Rather than dealing solely with existing cases of abuse and torture, Amnesty has developed a large and influential program for human rights education (Flowers 2002). More importantly, Amnesty is not unique in this regard. Traditional development organi-

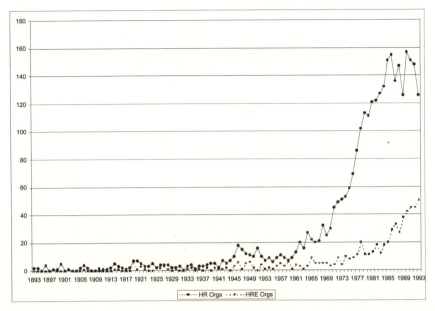

Figure 4.3.

zations and older human rights organizations also have altered their mission to support human rights education (Nelson and Dorsey 2003). Many human rights organizations now focus on education, and a number of traditional education and development organizations have also started to adopt human rights concepts (Flowers 2002). Human rights education has expanded in relevance and visibility, and this expansion has involved both the creation of new organizations and the transformation of older organizations.

Around the time of the UNESCO Recommendation, organizations and individuals throughout the world also began to publish materials on human rights education. By the mid-1990s enough materials were appearing that NGOs started to catalog the materials into bibliographies representing the publications of organizations throughout the world (Amnesty International 1992–1997; Elbers 2002). More recently, the United Nations also has started developing an international bibliography on human rights education (UN-HCHR 2003b).

Figure 4.4 presents a graph of these publications on human rights education by year and by major language category (English, Spanish, French, and Other). The number of publications for each language increases beginning in the late 1980s. As the graph indicates, in the 1980s the majority of the publications were in English, but toward the end of the decade other language

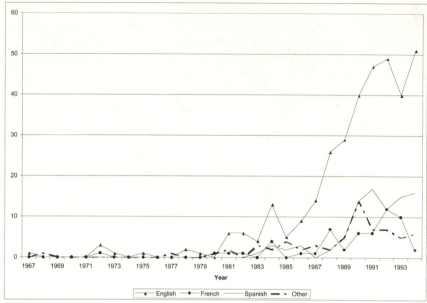

Figure 4.4.

groups began to produce human rights education materials as well. Many of these materials are available for free on the Internet, increasing the circulation of HRE resources and ideas available for classroom use. In addition, educators and researchers involved in publishing HRE materials often view these human rights issues as global and not just national. Almost all of the publications are presented as adaptable to different societies and populations. While the effort is not to make "one size fit all," there are a number of cases where materials get translated into different languages or adapted with only minor changes. Teachers are encouraged to make appropriate changes depending on the national context, but the consistent message is that *human rights are universal and should be respected throughout the world*. More than just an increase in the sheer number of organizations dedicated to education, these publications demonstrate that organizations actively work to train new educators and teach the idea that human dignity and human rights are not bounded by the nation-state.

Finally, as human rights education has become more formalized and distinct as a field, individuals and organizations have developed "virtual networks" for communication and support. Beyond being a resource for HRE materials, the Internet serves to link human rights educators throughout the globe. Human Rights Education Associates (HREA 2004) is an international

NGO with a listserv where educators discuss issues important to the human rights education community. In the last few years participants have discussed definitions of HRE, pedagogy for human rights education, and assessment methods for HRE programs. These networks exist at both global and regional levels. The Inter-American Institute of Human Rights has a human rights education listserv for Spanish speakers, in which participants have a chance to communicate and interact with educators in other countries. These networks facilitate collaboration and innovation and they help link organizations for advocacy efforts.

Asia does not have a regional cultural organization, but this did not stop NGOs in the region from creating the Asian Human Rights Charter. According to the Charter, "thousands of people from various Asian countries participated in the debates during the three-year period of discussion on this document. In addition, more than two hundred nongovernmental organizations (NGOs) directly took part in the drafting process" (AHRC 2004, 37). Although the Charter was focused on human rights in general, the final document mentions that "Governments, NGOs and *educational* institutions should co-operate in disseminating information about the importance and content of human rights" (AHRC 2004, 25, emphasis added). Organizations at the local, national, and international levels are advocating for human rights education, and a variety of networks are engaging in empowering activities designed to get different groups to work together.

Beginning with the World Conference on Human Rights in Vienna in 1992, intense lobbying by NGOs like the People's Decade for Human Rights Education (Koenig 2002) culminated in the United Nations Decade for Human Rights Education. Lobbying for the UN Decade was a major effort made by NGOs to promote human rights education at the international level, and the UN Decade has been significant because it entails formal assessment and reporting requirements. UNESCO placed HRE on the international agenda in 1974, but in many respects the UN Decade resulted because of the work of NGOs and their efforts to hold the United Nations accountable to their earlier proclamations. In turn, the United Nations has started to assess the status of HRE throughout the world.

In the roughly thirty-year span between the founding of the United Nations and the UNESCO Recommendation in 1974, NGOs worked on human rights and human rights education at the national level and in grassroots communities. As the human rights movement became more institutionalized and visible, the formal education system became a primary target for human rights education. Since the United Nations Decade did not constitute a binding agreement for nations, many NGOs refocused their advocacy efforts on the national level following their success with lobbying the United Nations. In the midterm (five-year) report on the Decade, the United Nations commented that "Both the United Nations and its Member States have repeatedly recognized the invaluable contribution of non-governmental organizations to human rights education. The present review reconfirms that non-governmental organizations are key actors in that field" (United Nations 2000, 20). These organizations continue to work tirelessly on human rights education and their efforts demonstrate that HRE is not just a movement occurring at the level of discourse in national ministries and intergovernmental organizations.

Human Rights Education and Nations

Nations vary widely in their support of human rights education. There is variation within regions, between regions, and among countries. Some countries like Costa Rica have included human rights in the education curriculum since the early 1990s (Suarez 2006a), and some countries still have absolutely no mention of the topic at all in the curriculum. While some countries just sign international treaties supporting human rights education, other countries mention the importance of human rights education in national constitutions or mandate that human rights education be taught in classrooms. In spite of these variations, the direction is growth in interest. The overall pattern shows growth in the interest in human rights education at the national level.

As part of the UN Decade for Human Rights Education, nations have to report on activities pertaining to HRE. In a report available on the Internet, the United Nations High Commissioner for Human Rights summarizes national initiatives undertaken since 1995 (UNHCHR 2003a). Even though not every country has reported and many countries have not reported since the Decade first started, a review of the document reveals the same trends found in IGOs and NGOs—an increase in the presence of human rights education. The document is divided by world regions (Africa, Arab Countries, Asia/Pacific, Europe and North America, and Latin America and the Caribbean), and there are concrete examples of national initiatives in every region. As just one example of many, the report on Morocco states that:

> The Government initiated in 1994 a partnership between the Ministry for Human Rights and the Ministry for Education with the aim to elaborate a National Programme for Human Rights Education. In this context, the following activities have been undertaken: revision of school textbooks to ensure accordance with human rights standards; training seminars for teachers and their supervisors; pilot-testing of the National Programme in both urban and rural areas of the country. Morocco further reported on the initiative to hold the first Arabic gathering on human rights education within the Decade, in cooperation with UNDP and UNESCO, which led to the adoption of the Rabat Declaration on the

elaboration of a regional strategy for human rights education (UNHCHR 2003a).

A number of studies of Latin America also suggest that more countries are including human rights education in the curriculum now than in previous years (IIDH 2000; Suarez 2006b). Some countries like Haiti and Honduras have done very little work to incorporate human rights education into the curriculum, but other countries like Peru and Mexico have made a number of changes in favor of human rights education. Overall, in Latin America and other regions the trend is clearly in the direction of incorporating human rights education into the curriculum.

More research on the incorporation of human rights education in individual nations and regions is greatly needed, both in longitudinal case studies and in international comparative studies. The United Nations will publish a final report after the end of the Decade, and this document should facilitate a number of cross-sectional and longitudinal comparisons. We anticipate that there will be cases where lobbying by NGOs has a direct impact on the incorporation of HRE into the curriculum, but we also anticipate that quantitative studies will demonstrate independent effects from the human rights movement and the expansion of education in general. As the human rights movement becomes more institutionalized and as educational systems expand to incorporate more groups, the likelihood increases that more nations will integrate human rights education into national curricula.

HUMAN RIGHTS EDUCATION, SOCIALIZATION, AND CITIZENSHIP

Schools have always had a broader mission than the teaching of reading, writing, and arithmetic (Tyack 1966, 2003; Butts 1980). That broader mission has been to instill in students a set of values and norms that would facilitate their becoming good members of their national societies. There is well-established literature on the political agenda of schools, with both a more functionalist (Dreeben 1968) and a more critical tone (Bourdieu and Passeron 1977; Bernstein 1975). Much of this literature emphasizes the curriculum as the principal mechanism through which political socialization takes place. Whether one thinks of the curriculum in general or more specifically of civic education, what is learned in schools is imagined to reflect the national character and the prerequisites for participating in national society. Within this research, traditional curricular reforms are national exercises to realign school and classroom activities with national goals and interests.

More recently, comparative-educational sociologists have raised questions about the autonomy of nation-states and the distinctiveness of national educational goals and reforms. Within this emerging perspective, educational goals and curricular reforms are no longer solely national exercises. All sorts of exogenous or transnational influences are at work shaping educational enterprises across the world. Coercive, mimetic, and normative processes are emphasized in varying degree throughout this literature (DiMaggio and Powell 1983). Some comparative case studies have examined the ways local actors or specific nation-states react to external educational agendas (Arnove and Torres, 1999; Popkewitz, 2000). These studies are especially useful in identifying and making sense of different educational outcomes. Other studies focus on similar educational outcomes and link these developments to the rise and impact of cultural globalization. These studies stress how a world logic of appropriateness leads to educational isomorphism across countries, despite much cross-national variation in economy, polity, and culture (Meyer and Ramirez 2000; Ramirez and Meyer, 2002).

This chapter addresses why human rights education has grown so dramatically not just within the world of human rights organizations but also within educational systems throughout the world. HRE is an unexpected development since it clearly goes beyond the older and more limited notions of national citizenship. It also extends beyond the earlier and again more restricted view of human rights as a solely legal issue. Note that most national legal issues do not become transnational curricular matters. So, what kinds of world developments facilitate the emergence of human rights education throughout much of the world?

First, a world rigidly organized around an interstate system in which state sovereignty is the highest standard undergoes significant erosion. This initially takes the form of world models of citizenship rights that all proper nation-states should articulate, but increasingly a human rights discourse gains center stage. It will not do to simply state that a good country must extend equal citizenship rights to women; it is now imperative to assert that women's rights are *human rights*, as are the rights of children, gays and lesbians, disabled persons, immigrants, and indigenous peoples and ethnic minorities.

Second, the world must be more than fixated on education as economic investment; all sorts of problems and all sorts of solutions must be deeply rooted in education. It is not just economists who roam the world providing advice on how to fix education. A much broader range of educational expertise is evident in international governmental and nongovernmental organizations.

Third, the universalistic assumption of human rights goes hand in hand with the universalistic aspirations of educational expertise. Cross-national studies of curricular developments clearly show decreasing variability in curricular categories (Meyer, Kamens, and Benavot 1992), increasing salience of individual-centric social studies (Wong 1992), and the emergence of postnational citizenship in civic education (Rauner 1998). These longitudinal studies indicate a greater degree of curricular standardization than that which characterized earlier eras when curricular matters more exclusively reflected local concerns. Furthermore they reveal the emergence of an orientation in which the world and world standards become the proper object of study. For better or for worse, in the contemporary world educational experts activate world standards through the universalism of educational science. Lastly, an enormous amount of confidence in the efficacy of education must be firmly entrenched. The failure of educational reforms leads to alternative educational reforms, not a loss of faith in education.

Bearing these world developments in mind, it is perhaps not so surprising that the worldwide rise of a human rights discourse would include human rights education. Respect for human rights is increasingly becoming a standardized goal for a proper nation-state, quite apart from its human rights practices. In a world in which nation-states are attuned to what constitutes a proper nation-state, the articulation of appropriate goals is to be expected. As one researcher noted, "Usually, new curricula or innovations struggle to achieve recognition and legitimation. Human rights education, however, has both recognition and legitimation at the highest levels of government in a variety of international fora" (Tarrow 1992, 31). As human rights become more institutionalized at the global level, and as education expands to incorporate more groups and increase the authority of individuals, we anticipate that human rights education will continue to increase in prevalence in the curriculum.

CONCLUSION

In the last half century there has been an explosion in worldwide organizations and discourse on behalf of ever-expanding conceptions of human rights. This broad movement has resulted in an increase in (a) the number of groups whose human rights are to be protected, such as women and children, gays and lesbians, or ethnic minorities and indigenous peoples. It has also produced an increase in (b) the range of topics covered, such as basic due process rights, rights to an elementary and secondary education, rights to health, and rights to one's language and culture. It has expanded (c) the scope of human rights treaties and the number of countries that have ratified them. Finally, it has expanded (d) the density of organizational structures around the world engaged in advocacy, monitoring, and representation. This broad movement has affected policy and practice throughout much of the world. (See Ramirez and Meyer 2002 for a general sketch of research directions in this area; Wotipka and Ramirez 2003 for a specific analysis of the Convention to Eliminate All Forms of Discrimination against Women.)

The educational impact of the human rights movement is very great though not much theorized. Older notions of citizenship education or civics instruction now appear to be limited and outdated, if these are solely informed by older notions of citizenship rights. Thus, traditional civics education is clearly not a main current focus—indeed, some of the curricular time devoted to this subject may well be shifted to the new domain of HRE. The rights of minorities, women, and immigrants are now much more likely to be framed and understood in broader and universalistic human rights terms (see Soysal 1994 on the rights of "guest workers" in Western Europe). It seems likely that some of the older civics topics will receive less attention, relatively or absolutely, than they did when the national state and society were the exclusive focus of education for public life.

The worldwide human rights movement is a recent phenomenon, and an important foundation of human rights education. Human rights education has expanded dramatically since the mid-1970s, and the United Nations Decade for Human Rights Education has drawn even more attention to the movement. The growth in education and the variety of communities and identities represented in schools, combined with globalization and the success of the human rights movement, accounts for the strength and the success of human rights education at the global level.

NOTE

1. World society theorists have spent decades investigating how world cultural models shape nation-states. These scholars have investigated the impact of globalization on mass education (Meyer, Ramirez, and Soysal 1992), environmental policy (Frank et al. 1997), the political incorporation of women (Bradley and Ramirez 1997; Ramirez, Soysal, and Shanahan 1997; Ramirez and Wotipka 2001), and science (Schofer et al. 2000).

BIBLIOGRAPHY

Amnesty International. 1992, 1993, 1995, 1996, 1997. *Human Rights Education Bibliography, Vol. 1–5*. London, England: Amnesty International.

Arnove, Robert F., and Carlos Alberto Torres. 1999. *Comparative Education: The Dialectic of the Global and the Local*. Lanham, MD: Rowman & Littlefield.

AHRC [Asian Human Rights Commission]. 1998. "Our Common Heritage: Asian Human Rights Charter." Hong Kong: Asian Human Rights Commission.

Bernstein, Basil. 1975. *Class, Codes, and Control* (3 vols.) London: Routledge and Kegan Paul.

Bourdieu, Pierre, and J. C. Passeron. 1977. *Reproduction in Education, Society and Culture*. Beverly Hills, CA: Sage.

Bradley, Karen, and Francisco O. Ramirez. 1996. "World Polity and Gender Parity: Women's Share of Higher Education, 1965–1985." *Research in Sociology of Education and Socialization* 11: 63–91.

Branson, Margaret, and Judith Torney-Purta. 1982. *International Human Rights, Society, and the Schools*. Washington, DC: National Council for the Social Studies.

Buergenthal, Thomas, and Judith V. Torney. 1976. *International Human Rights and International Education*. Washington, DC: U.S. National Commission for UNESCO.

Butts, R. Freeman. 1980. *The Revival of Civic Learning: A Rationale for Citizenship Education in American Schools*. Bloomington, IN: Phi Delta Kappa Educational Foundation.

Claude, Richard Pierre. 1997. "Global Human rights Education: The Challenges for Nongovernmental Organizations." In *Human Rights Education for the 21st Century*, ed. George Andreopoulos and Richard Pierre Claude.

DiMaggio, Paul, and Walter Powell. 1983. "The Iron Cage Revisited: Institutional Isomorphism and Collective Rationality in Organizational Fields." *American Sociological Review* 48: 147–60.

Dreeben, Robert. 1968. *On What is Learned in School*. Reading, MA: Addison-Wesley.

Elbers, Frank. 2002. *Human Rights Education Resource Book*. Cambridge, MA: Human Rights Education Associates.

Flowers, Nancy. 2002. "What is Human Rights Education?" Unpublished paper presented at the International Expert Meeting on Human Rights, Munich, Germany.

Frank, David, Ann Hironaka, and Evan Schofer. 2000. "The Nation-State and the Natural Environment over the Twentieth Century." *American Sociological Review* 65, no. 1: 96–116.

HREA [Human Rights Education Associates]. 2004. www.hrea.org

IIDH [Interamerican Institute of Human Rights]. 2000. *Experiencias de Educación en Derechos Humanos en América Latina*. San Jose, Costa Rica: Ford Foundation.

Keck, Margaret E, and Kathryn Sikkink. 1998. *Activists beyond Borders*. Ithaca, NY: Cornell University Press.

Koenig, Shula. 2002. Interview on file with author. See also: www.pdhre.org

Lauren, Paul Gordon. 2000. *The Evolution of International Human Rights*. Philadelphia: University of Pennsylvania Press.

Martin, J. Paul, Cosmas Gitta, and Tokunbo Ige. 1997. "Promoting Human Rights Education in a Marginalized Africa." In *Human Rights Education for the 21st Century*, ed. George Andreopoulos and Richard Pierre Claude.

Meyer, John W., David Kamens, and Aaron Benavot. 1992. *School Knowledge for the Masses.* Washington, DC: Falmer Press.

Meyer, John W., and Francisco O. Ramirez. 2000. "The World Institutionalization of Education," pp. 111–32. In *Discourse Formation in Comparative Education,* ed. J. Schriewer. Frankfurt: Peter Lang Publishers.

Meyer, John W., F. Ramirez, R. Rubinson, and J Boli-Bennett. 1977. "The World Educational Revolution," *Sociology of Education* 50, no. 4: 248–58.

Meyer, John W., Francisco O. Ramirez, and Yasemin Nuhoglu Soysal. 1992. "World Expansion of Mass Education, 1870–1980," *Sociology of Education* 65: 128–49.

Miller, Valerie. 2002. "Critical Pedagogy and HRE." Online discussion available at: http://www.hrea.org/lists/hr-education/markup/msg00963.html

Nelson, Paul J., and Ellen Dorsey. 2003. "At the Nexus of Human Rights and Development: New Methods and Strategies of Global NGOs." *World Development* 31, 12: 2013–26.

OAU [Organization of African Unity] 1981. "African Charter on Human and Peoples' Rights (Banjul Charter)." O.A.U. Doc. CAB/LEG/67/3 rev. 5:21 I.L.M. 58.

OAS [Organization of American States]. 1988. "Additional Protocol to the American Convention on Human Rights in the Area of Economic, Social, and Cultural Rights 'Protocol of San Salvador.'" San Jose, Costa Rica: Organization of American States.

Popkewitz, Thomas. 2000. "Globalization/Regionalization, Knowledge, and the Educational Practices: Some Notes on Comparative Strategies for Educational Research." In *Educational Knowledge*, ed. Thomas Popkewitz. New York: State University of New York Press.

Ramirez, Francisco O. 1987. "Institutional Analysis." In *Institutional Structure*, ed. G. Thomas, J. Meyer, F. Ramirez, and J. Boli. Newbury Park, CA: Sage.

Ramirez, Francisco O, and John W. Meyer. 2002. "National Curricula: World Models and National Historical Legacies," pp. 91–107. In *Internationalisation: Comparing Educational Systems and Semantics*, ed. M. Caruso and H. Tenorth. Frankfurt: Peter Lang.

Ramirez, Francisco O., and Christine Min Wotipka. 2001. "Slowly but Surely? The Global Expansion of Women's Participation in Science and Engineering Fields of Study, 1972–1992." *Sociology of Education* 74: 231–51.

Ramirez, Francisco O., Yasemin Soysal, and Suzanne Shanahan. 1997. "The Changing Logic of Political Citizenship: Cross-National Acquisition of Women's Suffrage, 1890–1990." *American Sociological Review* 62: 735–45.

Rauner, Mary. 1998. *The Worldwide Globalization of Civics Education Topics from 1955 to 1995.* Unpublished doctoral dissertation. School of Education, Stanford University.

Schofer, Evan, Francisco O. Ramirez, and John W. Meyer. 2000. "The Effects of Science on National Economic Development, 1970–1990." *American Sociological Review* 65: 877–98.

Schofer, Evan, and John W. Meyer. 2005. "The Worldwide Expansion of Higher Education in the Twentieth Century." *American Sociological Review* 70: 898–920.

Soysal, Yasemin Nuhoglu. 1994. *Limits of Citizenship: Migrants and Postnational Membership in Europe*. Chicago: University of Chicago Press.

Suarez, David. 2006a. "Promoting Civil Society through Schooling: Civic Education in Costa Rica and Argentina." Unpublished paper, School of Education, Stanford University.

———. 2006b. "Creating Global Citizens? Human Rights Education in Latin America and the Caribbean." Unpublished paper. School of Education, Stanford University.

Tarrow, Norma. 1992. "Human Rights Education: Alternative Conceptions." In *Human Rights, Education, and Global Responsibilities*, ed. James Lynch, Celia Modgil, and Sohan Modgil. Washington, DC: Falmer Press.

Tiberghien, Jennifer. 1997. *The Power of Unarmed Prophets: Non-governmental Organizations as Carriers of Human Rights Education*. Unpublished M.A. thesis: School of Education, Stanford University.

Torney-Purta, Judith. 1987. "Human Rights and Education Viewed in a Comparative Framework: Synthesis and Conclusions." In *Human Rights and Education*, ed. by Norma Tarrow. New York: Pergamon Press.

———. 1984. "Human Rights." In *Teaching for International Understanding, Peace and Human Rights*, ed. Norman J. Graves, O. James Dunlop, and Judith Torney-Purta. Paris: UNESCO.

Tyack, David. 2003. *Seeking Common Ground*. Cambridge, MA: Harvard University Press.

Union of International Associations. Various years. *Yearbook of International Organizations*. Munich, Germany: K. G. Saur.

UNESCO [United Nations Educational, Scientific, and Cultural Organization]. 2003a. Available at: http://databases.unesco.org/fileh/wwwi32.exe/[in=interro.in]/

———. 2003b. "UNESCO Associated Schools Project Network (ASPnet): Historical Review 1953–2003." Ref:ASPnetCongressWD5–23.

———. 2002. "UNESCO Associated Schools Project Network (ASPnet): List of Participating Institutions." ED 2002/WS/24, English

———. 1974. "Recommendation Concerning Education for International Understanding, Co-operation and Peace and Education relating to Human Rights and Fundamental Freedoms." Available at: http://www.unhchr.ch/html/menu3/b/77.htm

———. 1971. "The Associated Schools Project in Education for International Cooperation and Peace." ED/MD/19, English

———. 1954. "Education for International Understanding and Cooperation. Programme of Coordinated Experimental Activities in Schools of Member States, Report on Activities in 1954." UNESCO/ED/141, English.

United Nations. 2000. "Report of the United Nations High Commissioner for Human Rights on the mid-term global evaluation of the progress made towards the achievement of the objectives of the United Nations Decade for Human Rights Education." Document A/55/360.

———. 1998. "The United Nations Decade for Human Rights Education 1995–2004" HR/PUB/Decade/1998/1. New York: United Nations.

———. 1948. *Universal Declaration of Human Rights*. U.N.G.A. Res. 217A (III), 3(1) UN GAOR Res. 71, UN Doc. A/810.

———. 1945. *Charter of the United Nations*. Available online at: http://www.un.org/aboutun/charter/

UNHCHR [United Nations High Commissioner for Human Rights]. 2003a. Untitled resource available at: http://193.194.138.190/html/menu6/1/initiatives.htm

———. 2003b. Untitled resource available at: www.unhchr.ch/hredu.nsf/

Wiseberg, Laurie S., and Harry M. Scoble. 1981. "Recent Trends in the Expanding Universe of NGOs Dedicated to the Protection of Human Rights." In *Global Human Rights: Public Policies, Comparative Measures, and NGO Strategies*, ed. Ved P. Nanda, James Scarritt, and George W. Shepherd Jr. Boulder, CO: Westview Press.

Wong, Suk-Ying. 1992. "The Evolution and Organization of the Social Science Curriculum." In *School Knowledge for the Masses*, by John W. Meyer, et al. Washington, DC: Falmer Press.

Wotipka, Christine Min, and Francisco O. Ramirez. 2003. "World Society and Human Rights: An Event History Analysis of the Convention on the Elimination of all Forms of Discrimination against Women." In *The Global Diffusion of Markets and Democracy*, eds. Beth Simmons, Frank Dobbin, and Geoffrey Garrett. Cambridge, UK: Cambridge University Press.

Zimmerman, Jonathan. 2002. *Whose America? Culture Wars in the Public Schools*. Cambridge, MA: Harvard University Press.

5

Europe as a Bazaar

A Contribution to the Analysis of the Reconfiguration of Nation-States and New Forms of "Living Together"

António M. Magalhães and Stephen R. Stoer

European space, and the political construction of Europe, is increasingly subject to a process of heterogenization that is caught between two logics. One is based on the "modern" logic of homogeneity that implies thinking Europe as a large nation-state (in competition with other large nation-states), and the other is based on what one might term a bricolage concept of unity where Europe is thought of as unity on the basis of diversity. This latter logic points to a Europe in which differences come together attempting to communicate on the basis of their apparent incommensurability and not on the basis of an equally apparent shared European heritage. In another work (Stoer and Magalhães, 2001), we have referred to this coming together through the use of the metaphor of the bazaar as a "territory." The bazaar is not a place of the mere exchange of commodities, although obviously it is important in this sense. This exchange is only one of the motives for the existence of the bazaar; it is also a meeting place for differences and for negotiation between them. In this process of negotiation, there is no privileged actor, or difference. All actors, including ourselves, constitute differences. This chapter will develop further this notion of the bazaar as the reconfiguration of relationships within and between modern nation-states. It will ask how forms of nation-state fragmentation and supranational fabrication/construction are related to processes of European construction and new forms of "living together."

FROM UTOPIAS TO HETEROTOPIAS: REINVENTING LIVING TOGETHER

Looking for the ideal way to live together is not typical of modernity. Plato, in the *Republic*, and St. Augustine, in the *City of God*, provide two examples of a search for the ordering of human societies on the basis of a particular organizing principle in an epoch much earlier than that of modernity. In the former, human order should reflect the order of truth and, in the latter, the supremacy of the divine. Later, to cite a few others, Thomas Campanella, in the *Civitas Solis,* Francis Bacon, in *New Atlantis*, Thomas Moore, in *Utopia*, Samuel Butler, in *Erewhon* and Cyrano de Bergerac in *Histoire Comique ou Voyage dans la Lune* attempted to design societies that did not exist anywhere, that is, utopias, in the literal sense of the term.

What modernity may have brought that was new, in this anxiety to create and think the ideal social order, was, if one can put it this way, its *scientization*. Modern utopias, as projects for social order, frequently take science as the basis of their legitimization. Comte dreamt of a republic where science would be the grand organizer and Marx conceived of the construction of communist society based on the science of historical materialism. In this sense, modern utopias, as conceptions of how one can live together, arise as a peculiar mixture of *transparent places* and *non-places* (Magalhães and Stoer, 2003b): *non-places* because they are defined as existing beyond the differences between individuals and groups; *transparent places* because their sociological character is defined, in the last analysis, on the basis of their scientific character.

"From each according to his own possibilities, to each according to his own needs" was the organizing principle of living together in communist utopia. This stage represented the kind of development toward which humanity progressed, crushing, in its path, developmental differences. In the *Grundrisse*, Marx, while discussing the Asiatic mode of production, assumed implicitly that the "normal" course of history was that of the West—more precisely that of Germany, Great Britain, and France. The Asiatic mode of production, of feudal origin, would perish under the weight of history—which would lead to capitalism and, on the basis of capitalism, to communism. In his wake, Lenin and the Bolsheviks, after having accomplished the 1917 Revolution and caught up in the contradiction of constructing a postcapitalist society in a feudal, agrarian, and premodern context, invented a new "stage," the NEP, in order to put the revolution back on track toward a society based on soviets. The grandeur of the great socialist utopia legitimized, via its very audacity, the massacre of the peasants, thus cancelling out this leftover from premodern history.

Effectively, modernity and nation-states, as we stated in another work (Stoer, Rodrigues, and Magalhães, 2003)—in line with the Fordist *accumulation* of capital—made "more of the same" the sociological compass of their organization—and modernists, who dreamt of the ideal social order, made utopia the site, par excellence, of "sameness." Not that the great utopias did not have a place to attribute to differences, but that, precisely, they conceived of such a place on the basis of its sameness, to which differences would be attributed. The criteria of attribution of a legitimate place for differences varied from the *ethnocentric* model—that viewed the other as different due to his/her (retarded) state of cognitive and cultural development—to the *generosity* model, which argued that the other's difference should be assumed, with all its consequences (for example, allowing totally uncontrolled immigration to Europe from all parts of the world), as a construction of the West itself. On the way, the *tolerance* model also appeared, as recognition of the difference of the other as long as the West itself defined this difference and its degree of proximity.

What all these models share in common is their classificatory and passive character with regard to difference. Western culture lived for centuries—with rare critical intervals—a kind of autocontemplation of its own ethical and political superiority. This superiority was justified in the most diverse ways, from the religious narrative—that affirmed the superiority of our God above all others—to the eventually more sophisticated philosophical narrative that justified the Western model as the realization by history of the universal spirit, as in Hegel. The tendency was always to postulate our own way of thinking and knowing as the most universal (and, therefore, the most correct) and our own way of political and social organization as the most "developed." Other epistemologies and social organizations—differences—were judged on the basis of this posture.

The critical consciousness of the acquisitions of the social and human sciences has been translated into theoretical and practical proposals that have been mainly organized on the basis of relativism. Still, that which is normally designated as such does not appear to be totally determined by the contextual character of the social practices of cultural frames (including, obviously, knowledge). Firstly, because the cultural framing of knowledge does not make of it something totally relative (Spiro, 1998), for example, all human beings of all cultures recognize that if one perforates the belly with a knife, and that if the cut is sufficiently deep, one's life is at risk. Secondly, because although the isolation of cultural differences in their own specificity may resolve the problem of specificity, it does not resolve the problem of their basic relational character.[1] In other words, if relativism corresponds above all to the consciousness of the incommensurability of difference, the critique of relativism means emphasizing the relational character of difference. From our point of view, it is at the crossroads of these two perspectives that one should place the attempt to think of differences; that is, at the intersection of the critique of ethnocentrism and of the critique of relativism (comparatively, see Stoer and Magalhães, 2001).

Indeed, the self-confidence of the West has come to be challenged in a movement where we look into the mirror of our own civilizational process. One of the indicators that we could select to illustrate the way in which European society and culture have traveled up to this moment of civilizational insecurity are what we call the four models of the conceptualization/ legitimization of difference (internal and external)—which, we argue, European society and cultural have developed (see table 5.1).

These four models are analytical in nature and were constructed in sequence. In this way, their content is frequently mixed and they do not exist per se; that is, they are activated in given contexts articulating at the same time the logics of the different actors involved and the structural factors which frame their action. Therefore, it is crucial to remember that the creation of these models includes the following questions: What is it that is behind the proposal for multiculturalism when it claims that "we should tolerate those who are different"? Is it only a moral question? Who should tolerate whom? Is this the solution offered by a state that has as its mandate to guarantee the social well-being in the context of organized capitalism? And what is behind the statement that "difference is us"? Flexible capitalism? The growing individualization of social subjects? Growing personal, group, and institutional reflexivity?

To speak of the recognition of difference without taking into account redistributive educational and social policies would appear to indicate falling into the trap of flexible capitalism (Rorty [1999] accuses the American left of having done precisely this). On the other hand, to speak of redistribution without taking into account the recognition of differences in all their incommensurability means remaining prisoner of a statist conception of citizenship, of being unable to live together comfortably with the claim "Difference is us!"

With regard to their implications for education, effectively, the *ethnocentric* model of relationship with difference, inspired by the Reason of the Enlightenment, founded an education sure of itself with regard to the transmission of values and of knowledge assumed to be indisputable and universal. The national curriculum and its respective disciplines reflected this self-assuredness and considered that the educational process was, undeniably, the process by way of which children and youth became "civilized" and integrated into Western culture. Being, par excellence, monocultural in its approach, any form of inter/multicultural education is totally rejected by this model.

The *tolerance* model is also reflected in a clear way in the structuration of education in European societies, giving origin to what has been termed benign educational multiculturalism. This model, on the basis of the notion of handicap—above all the cultural handicap of the children and youth of ethnic

Table 5.1. Four Models of the Conceptualization/Legitimization of Difference

Ethnocentric Model: The other is different due to his/her state of development—both cognitive and cultural	Founded on the "good" civilizational conscience of the West. Not only is the other judged on the basis of the established canons of that which is normal, normality itself becomes normative; that is, a way of thinking, living, and organizing the life of Western societies is obviously postulated as superior to other societies and cultures. History becomes, thus, a process of civilizational judgment based on a fixed starting point: WSMCHUC (Whites, Socially organized by the state, Masculine, Christian, Heterosexual, and with a tendency to be Urban and Cosmopolitan).
Tolerance Model: The other is recognized as different, but his/her difference is read through a standard that determines which difference is legitimate (to be tolerated)	The presence of others is recognized both within Western societies and outside of them. As the other is no longer susceptible to being located colonially and exotically outside Western conviviality, it becomes urgent that he/she be attributed a "place." The culture of tolerance arises as the action of he/she who tolerates with regard to he/she who is tolerated, the latter becoming therefore the object of the political and moral action that "places" him or her among "we." The Christian and humanist inspiration at the base of this model is not sufficient to hide the ethical and epistemological arrogance of he/she who claims to tolerate.
Generosity Model: The other is different and this difference is taken on as the West's own construction.	Founded on the guilt of the West as a social paradigm. The comfortable world that the West has constructed for itself, within walls, makes those who live there feel guilty for the desolate lives lived by the others. Guilt, via the self-critique that lies at its base, becomes a political program: care for the other. The problem of the other is our problem, given that historically the other was continuously scorned. It is suggested that the other's emancipation will lead to our own emancipation. In this sense, those without voice are obligated to speak, even if they don't want to.
Relational Model: The other is different and so are we! Difference is in the relation between those who are different.	Refuses both the good conscience and the guilt shackled to the zero-sum game, asking Who has been most oppressed and who has been more the oppressor? Us and Them are part of a relation, which makes our own position more fragile—we are no longer the "we" that have the universal legitimacy to determine who "they" are. But in assuming that difference is also apparent of us ("we" become "they"), it is our own difference that is exposed by the relation with the other. Unilateral action with regard to difference is rejected, no matter how generous it may be, as if difference had a nature that should be cared for and deployed by us.

minorities and of the working classes (differently from compensatory education which has its basis in a social handicap and which is encompassed by the ethnocentric model)—contemplates cultural and pedagogical compensation of such children and youth via the action of an inter/multicultural education promoted by the school and by teachers. To be tolerant is, in this sense, to recognize difference without wishing to know it or, in other words, to wish to *resolve* the question of difference by way of a concern with *lifestyles*, relegating *life chances* to second place.

The *generosity* model is the model that has probably gone furthest in its relationship to difference in the field of education, until now. One is dealing, effectively, with a proposal for the construction of a critical inter/multicultural education, which struggles against the reduction of difference to its folkloric component and which opposes itself to benign inter/multicultural education. In this sense, it promotes the development of pedagogic differentiation devices capable of including as fully as possible precisely those that the school has contributed to excluding. Here, instead of a *resolution* of the question of difference via educational techniques imbued with instrumental rationality, the necessity to *build bridges* between cultures conceptualized as "incomplete" is taken on. The other has to be known through education and not simply recognized and, further, knowledge of the other functions as an emancipatory self-knowledge.

The *relational* model, founded on the assumption that "difference is us," appears to contain rich potential for rethinking inter/multicultural education. To start with, it takes as its starting point the proposal that difference should be thought of in all its incommensurability; that is, in assuming that difference is also us (thus transforming "us" into "them"), it is our own otherness that is exposed in the relationship. Thus, it is otherness that takes on agency and becomes proactive. With respect to inter/multicultural education, this may imply that one is *simultaneously on the bridge and at its margins*. In other words, inter/multicultural education manifests itself as being, on the one hand, the place of the encounter/confrontation of differences and of their negotiation and, on the other, the place that is itself agencied by difference. That is, it is schooling itself that is placed on the trajectories of social and cultural agents and not the other way around. Our difference is expressed via inter/multicultural education not as that education that brings with it illumination—the 'right' model, generosity—but rather as that education that brings with it its own difference. The margins on our side, on the side of our difference, can be translated into a project of the management of difference, but never into a project of its domination for that would be equivalent to negating our own difference.

It is on the basis of this act of making relative our own "we" that inter/ multicultural education might be reconfigured, situating itself on the razor's edge, that is, as we stated above, locating itself at the intersection of the critique of ethnocentrism and of the critique of relativism. The curricula, the devices, and the processes of teaching/learning would need to reflect this perspective according to which one assumes, relationally, the incommensurable difference of others and of our own. At the same time, they must be wary of falling prey to voluntarism or ingenuousness, for example, in relation to the extremely selective characteristics of new labor markets.

THE "REBELLION OF DIFFERENCES" AND THE BAZAAR OF KUWAIT

Behind the relational model and its appeal for heterotopias lies, what we have termed in another work (Stoer and Magalhães, 2001) the "rebellion of differences." In sum, the rebellion of differences refers to the fact that differences have rebelled against the cultural, political, and epistemological of Western modernity. They refuse to be seen as passive objects to be known, like the "primitive" that Anthropology took as its object of study; like the subject "without history" that many historians determined as such; like the individual "without state" that urged to be politically developed, such as the mythico-magical thinker that waits for the intellectual favors of scientific thought; and like the prisoner of the concrete that psychology opposed to the riches of abstract thought.

As suggested above, differences have taken on agency and no longer passively accept even the most generous discourses made about them (and often made on their own behalf!). Differences have begun to assume themselves as the subjects of their own enunciations, that is, as the subjects of discourses about themselves. And, furthermore, this discourse (*by* difference and not *on* difference) cannot be unified in a coherent narrative in which all "others" can recognize and affirm themselves. What characterizes differences and their relationships today are precisely their heterogeneity and their unfailing resistance to any sort of epistemological or cultural domestication. Western culture arises here, then, as difference itself and not as some standard on the basis of which other differences can be defined and judged.

With this rebellion of differences, all seems to take place as if the ideal organizing principle for living together had, on the one hand, multiplied and diversified itself into myriad ideal orders, or heterotopias. On the other, it is as if these heterotopias were designed as being ineluctably incommensurable. Differences, in fact, in their incommensurability of gender, ethnicity, lifestyles, and so forth, do not take on as part of their agenda either a universal common principle or a common political program.[2] It is as if the ideal of revolution or of reform (reform being, in a *petite histoire*, a revolution; and revolution being, in a *grande histoire*, a reform) had multiplied exponentially.

Authors such as Santos (1994) have directed attention to the closing off of social movements in mini-rationalities, or in rationalities that are minimum (Mohanty, 1989), and sociologists such as Archer (1991) have denounced the postmodern perversion of the dangerous division of humanity into humanities. Still, it is not enough to verbally exorcise the wasting away of humanity, and its Utopia, in an outcry for common political emancipation or for one sociology for one whole world. What must be brought to the front stage is that which, eventually, is susceptible of being recognized as common.

In a well-known debate between the philosopher Richard Rorty and the anthropologist Clifford Geertz on the organization of modern Western societies, the latter proposes the metaphor of the *bazaar of Kuwait* in order to account for the simultaneous tendency for fragmentation and for aggregation in these societies. Geertz talks concretely about how in an epoch of globalization local communities increasingly appear to be an enormous *collage*, that is, in each one of its localities, the world seems increasingly more to be like "a Kuwaiti bazaar than an exclusive English club" (cited by Rorty, 2000). This latter represents the incommensurability of local and cultural differences: the *portugueseness* of the Portuguese, the *englishness* of the English, the *arabic character* of the Arabs, and so on.

We wish to argue that it is on the basis of the idea that difference is agency and that the bazaar of Kuwait conveys the incommensurability of local and cultural differences—both acting as the structuring propositions for a new conception of societies and present sociabilities, that the idea of living together can be reinvented. With regard to the bazaar of Kuwait, a few explanatory words are in order. Thus, we conceive of this bazaar in the following terms:

1. It is a regulated public space (political, social, cultural . . .) that as such is susceptible to being regulated;
2. A public space possessed, and possesses, various configurations in different parts of the world, but the dominant configuration is that that results from it being structured by the state;
3. The modern state has been a potential disseminator of (in)justice;
4. If reconfigured, the state can be an important agent of the redistribution of social justice and of the dissemination of the recognition of difference, as well as an important instrument in the implementation of distributive justice;

5. The sovereignty that "differences" demand from the state does not correspond to the dissolution of the state as agent of justice (above all distributive), but accepts the legitimacy of differences to regulate their own lives ("I pay my taxes [duty], but I want to educate my children [right] as I think they ought to be educated");

6. The bazaar, a regulated public space, is a place where redistributive justice and justice based on the recognition of differences constitute a variable geometry: the degree of variation depends on the degree of power and conflict that exists between differences;

7. This variable geometry is, at the same time, consensual and arbitrary, and therefore fragile;

8. This fragility and instability are not characteristics of a stage to be overcome, but, rather, a permanent state: democracy is no longer conceptualized as a stage of development, but as an end in itself (without end) (Santos, 1998).

This political definition of the bazaar rests on the idea that taking on the notion of difference as agency raises a question of power, emphasizing that differences affirm themselves as, in Wallerstein's words, "an ideological battleground," that is, making matters of discrimination, racism, and exclusion dialectic with those derived from inequality in the distribution of wealth. To unlink the elements of the triad "cultural power — affirmation of difference — economic equality" is to risk being deceived by modern strategies founded on the principle according to which social justice derives (more or less directly) from economic justice. We know, today, that it doesn't work that way: the struggle for social justice that has its origin in the affirmation of difference, in present social movements, does not arise separated from claims for economic justice, and vice versa. Furthermore, this latter now arises frequently reconfigured by the former.

THREE MODELS AND METAPHORS
FOR EUROPEAN CONSTRUCTION

If all language has a metaphorical origin (Ricoeur, w/d) and even the structure of scientific language can be said to be poetical, it can also be claimed that metaphors, in sociological terms, have consequences. That is, the terms in which the social is thought and spoken have repercussions on the nature of that same social. There are many examples, ranging from Spencer's biological metaphor to the more recent term *network*, used to designate a way in which groups and societies develop. In this chapter, although seeking by way of the bazaar metaphor to make things clearer and to promote analysis, we do not wish to become prisoners of this term. The bazaar has, on the one hand, a premodern connotation and, on the other, an exotic-romantic connotation which has little to do with our use of the term here.

Alain Mons states that

> the metaphoric process in its different expressions, in its crystallisation of the image, the territory, in communication, leads us to a fictional economy that increasingly outweighs a material economy. Today, which of the two determines the other? In fact, it is impossible to say, given that they perfectly intertwine in the complexity of their exchange. The visible metaphors of the 'fields' irresistibly project themselves towards a poetry of the social, through a collage-effect, through the overlapping of representations, through invisibility, virtuality, through the explosion of sense. (Mons, n.d., 8)

As we suggested above, the metaphor of the bazaar of Kuwait is indelibly marked by the locality that makes it up. The sounds, the smells, the diversity of motives that lead people there, make the *souk* a privileged metaphor, for there it is not only business and commercial transactions that are at stake but rather everything, or almost everything, that has to do with the social life of the population. In Fez, for example, the marketplace activity and the shops of artisans and merchants are accompanied by universities (*madras*), bridal processions on the back of a donkey, and other noncommercial events. It is in this sense of a totally social phenomenon that the bazaar is a metaphor with potentiality for rethinking Europe. Still, as a result of its bearing heavily the premodern characteristics of the market, and the social ties centered above all on the family and other traits of the precapitalist mode of production, the metaphor of the bazaar—in spite of our attempts to define its characteristics—may put at risk our purpose. Thus, in order to, in a manner of speaking, free ourselves from the metaphor itself, we shall try to give it a content more adequate to that which we have in mind by confronting it with other perspectives.

Europe as the State of Nationalities and a Temptation of the Past

The Europe of nations exists and it is undeniable that there is a claim on the part of some for a corresponding state and, on the part of others, for institutions that allow them to express their proactive identity. The first case, that of nations seeking a state, is illustrated by the Basques and the Corse, to cite only these, and, in the second case, by Catalonia and the Flemish. And very recently we were witness to the violent claims of national affirmation made in the unmaking and remaking of Yugoslavia, a process that revealed itself, in some aspects, as a state in search of a nation. Nations and national claims for state construction are still an undeniable part of European reality with all the implications for identity construction that they imply.

In the case of the European Union, this dimension appears in apparently mitigated forms, by way of the *civilized* conflict for recognition of national languages as official languages, with regard to the rank in the list of European nations, that is, as a nation "in last place," "behind the Greeks," or "before the Germans." These are powerful political *tropos*. Knowledge of the process of the construction and consolidation of nation-states, above all European, allows one to take the position of not wishing to repeat the same errors, above all that error of, by chance, attempting to find in the nation-state model a model for Europe. As is well known, and in paraphrasing Stuart Hall (1992), the majority of nation-states came into being through a long process of violent conquest and/or suppression of cultural difference. Each conquest in the national saga led to the subjugation of conquered peoples and their cultures in an attempt to impose a more unified cultural hegemony (the case of English hegemony with regard to the United Kingdom comes immediately to mind). On the other hand, modern Western nations were the centers of empires or of neoimperial spheres of influence, exercising cultural hegemony over colonized cultures. Ingenuousness is something that is reflexively disallowed. Nobody today can enjoy the luxury of innocence: it is difficult to imagine European construction based on the affirmation of a father or mother land, of a religion (Christianity or otherwise), or of a language (either as a lingua franca—"European English"—or otherwise). Instead, the Europe of nations might be able to take advantage of the displacement and reconfiguration of political power toward another center—Brussels, Strasbourg—in order to reframe the case of Corsica, the Basques, the Belgians, etc., as new actors that exist beyond London, Madrid, and others.

On the one hand, say Held and McGrew, the skeptics "(f)ar from considering national governments as becoming immobilised by international imperatives, . . . point to their growing centrality in the active promotion and regulation of cross-border activity" (2002, 105). On the other hand, Hedley Bull emphasizes precisely the need to develop an alternative to state systems such as they are known today:

> I do not propose to speculate as to what these non-historical alternatives might be. It is clearly not possible to confine the varieties of possible future forms within any finite list of political systems, and for this reason one cannot take seriously attempts to spell out the laws of transformation of one kind of universal political system to another. [. . .] But our view of possible alternatives to the states system should take into account the limitations of our own imagination and our own inability to transcend past experience (2002, 466).

It is in this sense of the widening of sociological possibilities that it is important to confront other conceptions for the development of Europe to reconfigure the very structure of sovereignty of the nation-states. The future European Constitution (see *European Convention, Draft Treaty Establishing a Constitution for Europe*, 18 July 2003) finds itself, thus, in a very peculiar historical position, for its flaw may reside in the temptation to try to find in the past a model for the future. Thus, some speak of a Europe that goes as far as the Urals, while others limit it to Christianity, and even others refer to a version of Europe with borders drawn in the name of God.

The question of the political sovereignty of the European Union can already be considered on the basis of this apparent divergence between state systems of the past and a new emergent mode of sovereignty. This can be seen in the definition of "categories of competences" (article 11), of "exclusive competence" (article 12), and of "areas of shared competence" (article 13) (*European Convention*, 2003) of the *Proposal for a Constitution for Europe*, for the way in which the exercise of this sovereignty is being configured is to some extent exceptional. Citing Keohane, "the European Community is not by any means a sovereign state, although it is an unprecedented hybrid, for which the traditional conception of sovereignty is no longer applicable" (2000, 116). The same author emphasizes that what is at stake is a new form of interrelationship between different European nation-states, that is, interdependence "is characterized by continual discord within and between countries, since the interests of individuals, groups and firms are often at odds with one another" (Keohane 2000, 116).

It is for this reason that it is necessary to sift through the trunk of themes, or issues, that Mary Kaldor (1995) refers to as a possible basis for political identity, and to which we shall refer in the next section, in order to find some nourishment for the sociological imagination.

Europe as Issue-Based Rather than Territorially Based

Mary Kaldor defines four key characteristics of nation-states as a "particular form of the state that came into being during the nineteenth century": political identity—"based on *citizenship* which is linked to *territory*"; culture— "vertical and homogenizing"; money—"consist[ing] of a unified national currency issued by a *central bank*"; and organized violence—"tak[ing] the form of *national armies*, which represent[s] its only legitimate form" (1995: 71–73, emphasis in the original). According to Kaldor, "the nation-state had a short life," becoming evident in the latter half of the twentieth century that it was "too large to protect cultures . . . too large for efficient democratic decision-making . . . too small to regulate what had become a global economy, . . . [and] too small to prevent wars" (74–75). It was therefore replaced by what the same author terms a bloc system with the following characteristics: "political identity . . . based on national *membership* of the bloc, which in turn is based on *ideology* (i.e., a commitment to parliamentary democracy and capitalism in the West or to socialism in the East"; "a common *horizontal culture* linking elites"; a characteristic form of *money* that "for the Western bloc . . . was *hegemonic*"; and "armed forces . . . organized in *integrated command structures*" (75–76). With regard to the bloc system, which also had a short duration, Kaldor asks:

> In what sense did the blocs prefigure new state forms? They were not simply new coalitions of nation-states. In the notion of an ideological community, rather than a territorially based or culturally based community, in the *a priori* if not *de facto* universalism of the bloc, in the construction of new horizontal elite cultures, in the creation, in theory, of international money and, above all, in the limitations on national armed forces, the bloc system marked a decisive break with the nation-state (Kaldor, 1995, 77).

The information technology revolution of the 1970s and 1980s had an impact on the characteristics of forms of state power. Political identity in the form of "bloc identity . . . disappeared with the end of the Cold War"; culture became "transnational communication [that] makes possible all kinds of new horizontal networks, which are not necessarily elite networks"; hegemonic money was called into question and weakened by the "growth of international liquidity and the increase in the size and speed of capital flows"; and "the character of war [has] changed dramatically . . . [and t]he monopoly of organised violence is undermined both through transnationalization and privatization" and, paraphrasing Kaldor, war has become a global spectacle (Kaldor, 1995, 80–83).

Although Kaldor recognizes that European construction could mean reverting to nation-state forms of political organization, she argues that "in the post-bloc era [this] would be anachronistic and hazardous" (Kaldor, 1995, 69). She sets out two possible models for the future, one based on what would be a combination of the nation-state and bloc models and another based on a "new set of horizontal state structures." It is this latter model that may nourish our imagination for new possibilities with regard to European construction. The characteristics of this model are: political identity based on a "voluntary *membership* which is *issue based* rather than territorially based" (examples of such issues might be human rights, security, the environment, economic and financial management); culture horizontally based on "a commitment to solve certain shared global problems, i.e., green/peace/development/human rights"; money based on "a genuine form of international money guaranteed by international monetary institutions which are democratically accountable"; and organized violence based on "a series of interlocking security arrangements, including multinational units and a complex mutual inspection framework" that transform national armed forces into "cultural relics" (88).

In discussing issues or themes, one is not aiming at the recovery of proposals already elaborated by diverse analysts and sociologists, that often end up emptying such issues under the weight of a guiding theme, such as, for example, the "emancipation of humanity," the "conscientization of social subjects," or the "Utopia of equality." On the contrary, the issues arise here as hybrid forms of regulation and emancipation. It is not the superior character (in ethical or political terms) of the issue that legitimates it as such, but rather its capacity to bring together interests and desires (a voluntary association) that are on citizens' agendas and, as such, are claimed as important by them. These interests and desires do not always coincide with the utopic ideals inherited from the nineteenth century. They can also result from questions that have arisen in more recent times, such as the claim for the free circulation of people and commodities and the standardization of products and means of consumption in the name of efficiency and effectiveness. There is no a priori guarantee that a political measure within the scope of an issue or theme will be either emancipatory or regulatory in character. For example, the normalization of flushing cisterns in bathrooms can be seen as an intrusion of the bureaucrats of Brussels into one of the most intimate zones of our lives, or it can be seen as the rationalization of costs and control over the wastage of water. In an opposite sense, policies designed on the basis of an issue that is considered from the start as emancipatory, for example, the opening of green zones to the public as leisure zones, can produce the contrary, that is, the destruction of these same green zones leading once again to their being closed off to the public.

With regard to the cultural dimension referred to by Kaldor, challenges to patriarchalism, the affirmation of different lifestyles and the concern with ecology, arise not as European issues, per se, but with strong potential for the political aggregation of Europe. The themes of the fight against patriarchy, the concern with ecology, the claims of group and individual identity—both of a political dimension and of a cultural dimension—are the field, par excellence, of the new social movements that have a global dimension in both the wider and more restricted senses of the term. Given that Europe itself is also a question of identity and a question of belonging, whatever that may mean, the issues are clearly not enough to enable Europe to establish her own difference with relation to other spaces. Still, this difference is a possibility to be taken on as an option by the nation-states that wish to be part of Europe.

Unlike the national identities and histories, as they were codified in the ardent processes of state and nation building, Europe cannot afford to develop its discriminating particularisms and authentic markers. It derives its legitimacy from universalistic principles and from the future it projects. And that future, or aspiration for that future, is now entangled with others' futures, making European identity broader than Europe itself. (Soysal, 2003, 62)

This option to "be part of" arises as a reconfiguration of the nation-state, particularly with regard to sovereignty. Participation through issues, or themes, such as the Euro or defense of the environment, has as its counterpart in offering a part of oneself for the development of the issue, as is suggested by the principles of "concession," of "subsidiarity," and of "proportionality" inserted in the *Proposal for a Constitution for Europe* (art. 9).

It is in the apparent paradox between the universalist character of the issues of political identity and the "local" character of Europe that this latter can potentially affirm itself, on the one hand, via the reconfiguration of its international policy; that is, in not taking political action on the basis of the formation of blocs, be they Soviet, American, Asiatic, or other. Thus, as Habermas argues, the European Union can never have as its main objective a confrontation with American economic power, which would make its project "particularistic" (1999: 58). On the other hand, the participation of nation-states in the issues of political identity will lead, inevitably, to the unleasing of dynamics that will lead to their own reterritorialization. Given that territories are simultaneously real and virtual, it is possible and necessary to rethink the different policies (having to do with both difference and redistribution) on the basis of not only new territories (local, regional, supranational)—Europe, for example—but also deterritorialized territories. Thus, the issues of political identity can arise as forms of this type of deterritorialized territory: the environment, gender, human rights, common currency, free movment of persons and commodities, and so on. The nation-states voluntarily associated to the project, with regard to the issues, have the opportunity to reterritorialize themselves again on the basis of the reconfigurations demanded by their citizens (see, though, the concept of "demanded, or claimed, citizenship," Stoer and Magalhães, 2004).

Europe as a Network State

From what has been said so far, it appears clear that Europe arises for citizens, sociologists, and political action as something more *under construction* than actually *constructed*. The agency of social actors and their reflexivity are crucial for the agenda of Europe as a place of the most recent and stimulating sociological invention. It is in this sense that—before returning to the metaphor of the bazaar—we think it is important to consider Europe as one of the first *network states*.

Castells refers precisely to Europe as a network state since:

> there is one European state. It is not made up of the European Commission. The European Commission is a bureaucracy which many people hate and mistrust, and it clearly has no power. The power is in the European Council of Ministers, chiefs of Government of all countries meeting every three months, making decisions to be decided by the European Commission. It works . . . as a network state. It is the only explicit network state so far. The others are implicit. (Castells, 2001, 121)

Others, such as Nóvoa and Lawn, refer to the "fabrication of Europe" by way of a networking process, "linking social structures, networks and actors at the local, national and European levels," that may "describe and explore the formation of new European identities with emergent policy networks, leading to the emergence of the European education space, a fuzzy but significant concept in education policy" (2002, 4). In this sense, and as we have argued in another work (Stoer, Rodrigues, and Magalhães, 2003), Europe arises as a center for the coming together of multiple and diversified powers that are not simply based on powers emanating from national territories (and their globally informed hierarchies) but, rather, define themselves on the basis of identities.[3] Such powers are thus in conflict, not only among themselves, but also with regard to previously established logics, such as those defined by nation-state territories—for example, the process of the "greening of the self" enters into conflict with the established production, distribution, and consumption processes of the nation-state to which it belongs.

Carnoy, in the wake of Castells, in a recent work on "the role of the state in the new global economy (2001)," has begun conceptualizing the "network state." This is a state

> made up of shared institutions, and enacted by bargaining and interactive iteration all along the chain of decision-making: national governments, co-national governments, supra-national bodies, international institutions, governments of nationalities, regional governments, local governments and NGOs. . . . This new state functions as a network, in which all nodes interact and are equally necessary for the performance of the state's functions. It is a state whose efficiency is defined in terms of its capacity to create and sustain networks—global, regional and local networks—and through these networks, to promote economic growth and develop new forms of social integration. (Carnoy, 2001, 31)

These new forms of social integration, which indeed correspond to a new form of regulation, relate to two features. First, they result from the new role of knowledge in the productive process, "in creating conditions for economic growth . . . and in managing and compensating the [de-equalizing] effects of globalisation locally" (Carnoy, 2001, 31). Second, they provide the opportunity for the articulation of the network state with what we have termed in another work hybrid forms of regulation (Stoer and Rodrigues, 2000), due to the fact that they conflate a horizontal political logic with a vertical one. With regard to the former, what is at stake are largely the effects of the process of the translation of knowledge into competencies. In Stoer and Magalhães (2003; see also Magalhães and Stoer, 2003a), we develop this argument further as the reconfiguration of what a "mandate" in education may signify, in the context of a knowledge and information society where there occurs a simultaneous downward and upward pressure both on the nation-state and on nation-state citizens. With regard to the latter, at stake is the articulation of a space, where redistributive justice and the justice linked to the recognition of differences, with a state whose legitimacy has been challenged by important economic changes and the development of a new social ontology (Stoer, Rodrigues, and Magalhães, 2003). In other words, the rise of Europe as a network state apparently signifies the rise of a state that takes on the task of being capable of providing the conditions necessary for the development of a social policy that bases itself on the capacity of citizens to deal with the potentialities and risks inherent to flexible capitalism.

CONCLUSION: EUROPE AS A BAZAAR

The first of these three perspectives, the Europe of national identities, is characterized by a strong emphasis on territorialization and on its being founded on national identity (described almost always as homogeneous). The second perspective, the Europe of issues/themes, is characterized by a strong appeal for cosmopolitan and deterritorialized causes. The third perspective, the network state, underlines the centrality of the circulation of knowledge/information and, above all, the role of knowledge as a crucial factor in production. However, one still remains with the sensation that each of these perspectives offers to the construction of the political agenda for Europe that which the others in some way are unable to offer. It is in this sense that, in our view, the metaphor of the bazaar gains strength, precisely because it aims at taking on the dialectical combination and the whole of the combined effects of the three perspectives.

With regard to the first, we can state, paraphrasing A. Touraine, that the political agenda for European construction does not need to base its architecture on the model of the nation-state but, rather, on the basis of a state capable of managing the cultural wealth of its nations. The emphasis on national identity can be combined dialectically with the issues/themes of the second perspective. That is, if in the first the focus is on national territory and culture, in the second the agenda is enriched by its concerns with cosmopolitanism. For example, to be Portuguese cannot mean consciously "drowning" archaeological world heritage in name of the "interests" of Portugal, as in the case of Foz Côa, just as being Spanish or French cannot mean ignoring the ecological balance of the others' maritime waters. Frequently, the third perspective, that of the network state, is presented as the only and the most realistic perspective, mainly because informationalism and the knowledge society have become almost taken for granted or have become canon for development in the current context. In the sequence of the Lisbon Summit (2000), not only was knowledge brought forward with regard to the agenda setting of different policy sectors, but it also became, itself, a strong organizer of policy initiatives. To have a place in the European network became a primary aim to the extent that national scientific research agencies, in their institutional declarations, appeared to suggest that their very existence depended upon belonging to a network (*compare with* the process of the creation of European networks).

This perspective of Europe—as founded on knowledge as a central factor in production and on the circulation of information, both processes that are strongly deterritorialized—offers, in spite of its recent erosion by political rhetoric, numerous possibilities. Within the scope of education policy, for example, this centrality has become particularly evident, reconfiguring even the political mandate for education (Magalhães and Stoer, 2002). Still, it can be argued that these possibilities—instead of having been exploited through the implications of the reconfiguration of capitalism, where knowledge assumes a central place in the productive process—have led to a conceptualization of the network as a kind of transparent place, a meeting point of consensus and convergence for everything and everyone. We wish to argue that to be European, to be a citizen in this network state, can effectively mean more than the mere rescaling of attributed citizenship by the national states.

It is for this reason that it appears to make sense to use the metaphor of the bazaar in considering Europe and European construction. Europe as a bazaar, as we have already stated, corresponds to the emergence of a new form of regulation that congregates the contributions of the three perspectives for the conceptualization of Europe. The option for the use of the metaphor of the bazaar contains strong implications that derive from its own specific definition. These implications are centered, essentially, on the question of the relationship between redistributive justice and justice based on the recognition of difference and the question of the reconfiguration of citizenship. That is, the transformation of "attributed citizenship" into "claimed, or demanded, citizenship" (Magalhães and Stoer, 2003a), which, in its turn, implies the redesigning of the politics of difference based on the perspective identified above as "difference is us."

The conception of the bazaar, as a political metaphor for European construction, incorporates and mediates the three perspectives presented above for this construction and their founding metaphors—the flag, issues/themes, and the network—without losing its own specificity. That which the bazaar brings to the discussion as new and founded on the enunciation "difference is us," may be summed up in the following way:

1. It means the possibility of the rise of a state able to regain legitimacy through "facilitating the creation of new communities and new identities around these communities" (Carnoy, 2001: 32), in the sense that it is not possible to identify a privileged community as central actor of the new political spaces.[4]
2. Its political realization, as we emphasized above, is of a variable geometry, meaning that to the extent that it depends on the relationship between that which is consensual and that which is, eventually, arbitrary, its configuration is always fragile (see, for example, the use and abuse of the criteria for financial convergence by the more powerful member-states) and renegotiable.
3. The bazaar is not configured as an ossified structure, tending toward the fixation of harmonies; it is, rather, made up of continuous processes and unstable conflicts where negotiation and consensus will always occupy a central political place.

We bring this chapter to a close by underlining a doubt: Will Europe as a bazaar have what it takes to carry out the functions that the Europe of the flag, of the issues/themes, and of the network, promise to do so effectively? Will it be capable of developing as a political metaphor the feeling of belonging of the first, of promoting the universalist cosmopolitism of the second, and the forms of production capable of sustaining the diversified lifestyles and the sophisticated potential of the third? Obviously there is no clear answer to this question, but the idea of the bazaar appears to focus upon the discussion of the concern with new forms of citizenship, linked to the locality—but also of a global dimension, founded on the discourses of the first person, both singular and plural (the plurality and diversity of voices in the bazaar may not be synonymous with confusion, but express, rather, differences) and on the conviviality structured by differences themselves.

NOTES

1. As is the case with some strands of multiculturalism that, in their anxiety to underline cultural differences, eradicate their relational character, such as if a Gypsy born and raised in Portugal had more in common with a Gypsy living in Romania than with other Portuguese.

2. John Rex, in his classic piece on "the concept of a multicultural society" (1988), talks of a "secular civic culture as a common and necessary component of all cultures, in advanced industrial societies" (1988: 206). Thus, multiculturalism for Rex "can only be tolerated if it does not threaten a shared civic culture including, evidently, the idea of equality of opportunity." It is precisely this utopia of a "shared civic culture" that, in our view, differences reject. Rex's sophisticated thoughts on what might constitute a multicultural society are embedded in a modern view of rational industrial development. It is the critique of this view that lies at the base of the rebellion of differences. See also the critique by Parekh (2000) of what he terms "proceduralist and civic assimilation theories."

3. It is evident that one cannot be ingenuous with regard to the "fabrication" of a European education space. As R. Dale (2003) has emphasised, at the base of good intentions often lie interests linked to the reorganization of the productive system and its political implications.

4. This aspect is full of consequences for education due to the fact that this field is progressively escaping the educational action of the state in order to be transferred to the world of "formation" and the environment of the market. The challenge that confronts the network state is that of how to reposition itself with regard to the educational field. Eventually, its strategy may be one of promoting, for example, *lifelong education* as an alternative to *continuous formation*.

REFERENCES

Archer, Margaret (1991). "Sociology for One World: Unity and Diversity." *International Sociology* 6, no. 2, 131–48.

Bull, Hedley (2002). "Beyond the States Systems?" in *The Global Transformations Reader: An Introduction to the Globalization Debate*, ed. David Held and Anthony McGrew. Oxford, UK: Blackwell Publishers.

Carnoy, Martin (2001). "The Role of the State in the New Global Economy" in *Challenges of Globalisation*, ed. Johan Muller, Nico Cloete, and Shireen Badat. Cape Town: Maskew Miller Longman.

Castells, Manuel (2001). "Growing Identity Organically," in *Challenges of Globalisation*, ed. Johan Muller, Nico Cloete, and Shireen Badat. Cape Town: Maskew Miller Longman.

Dale, Roger (2003). "The Lisbon Declaration, the Reconceptualisation of Governance and the Reconfiguration of European Educational Space." Paper presented to RAPPE Seminar "Governance, Regulation and Equity in European Education Systems" at the Institute of Education, University of London, 20 March.

Habermas, Jurgen (1999). "The European Nation-State and Pressures of Globalization," *New Left Review* 235, 46–59.

Hall, Stuart (1992). "The Question of Cultural Identity," in *Modernity and Its Futures*, ed. Stuart Hall, David Held, and Tony McGrew. Cambridge, MA: Polity Press/Open University Press, 273–316.

Held, David, and Anthony McGrew (2002). *The Global Transformations Reader: An Introduction to the Globalization Debate*. Oxford, UK: Blackwell Publishers.

Kaldor, Mary (1995). "European Institutions, Nation-States and Nationalism," in *Cosmopolitan Democracy*, ed. Daniele Archibugi and David Held. Cambridge, MA: Polity Press, 68–95.

Keohane, Robert (2000). "Sovereignty in International Society" in *The Global Transformations Reader: An Introduction to the Globalization Debate*, ed. David Held and Anthony MacGrew. Oxford, UK: Polity Press.

Magalhães, António M., and Stephen R. Stoer (2002). *A Escola para Todos e a Excelência Académica*. Oporto: Profedições.

———. (2003a). "Performance, Citizenship and the Knowledge Society: A New Mandate for European Education Policy," *Globalisation, Societies and Education* 1, no. 1, 41–66.

———. (2003b). "A Reconfiguração do Discurso Político: É Possível Falar a Partir de um 'Não-Lugar' ou de um 'Lugar Branco'?" *A Página*, October.

Mohanty, S. P. (1989). "Us and Them: On the Philosophical Bases of Political Criticism," *Yale Journal of Criticism* 2, no. 2, 1–31.

Mons, Alain (no date). *A Metáfora Social: imagem, território, comunicação*. Porto: Rés Editora.

Nóvoa, António, and Martin Lawn (2002). *Fabricating Europe: The Formation of an Education Space*. Dordrecht: Kluwer Academic Publishers.

Parekh, Bhikhu (2000). *Rethinking Multiculturalism*. London: Macmillan.

Rex, John (1988). *Raça e Etnia*. Lisbon: Editorial Estampa.

Rorty, Richard (2000). "Sobre o Etnocentrismo: uma resposta a Clifford Geertz," *Educação, Sociedade e Culturas* 13, 213–24.

———. (1999). *Para Realizar a América. O Pensamento de Esquerda no Século XX na América*. Rio de Janerio: DP&A Editora.

Santos, Boaventura de Sousa (1994). *Pela Mão de Alice*. Porto: Edições Afrontamento.

Santos, Boaventura de Sousa (1998). *Reinventar a Democracia*. Lisboa: Fundação Mário Soares/Gradiva Publicações.

Soysal, Yasemin (2003). "European Identity and Narratives of Projection," in *European Studies at Oxford: Whose Europe? National Modules and the Constitution of the European Union*, ed. Kalypso Nicolaidis and Stephen Weatherill. Oxford, UK: Oxford University Press, 62–65.

Spiro, Melford E. (1998). "Algumas Reflexões sobre o Determinismo e o Relativismo Culturais com Especial Referência à Emoção e à Razão," *Educação, Sociedade & Culturas* 9, 197–230.

Stoer, Stephen R., and António M. Magalhães. (2001). "A Incomensurabilidade da Diferença e o Anti-anti-etnocentrismo," in *Educação e Diferença*, ed. David Rodrigues. Porto: Porto Editora, 35–48.

———. (2004). "Education, Knowledge and the Network Society," *Globalisation, Societies and Education* 2, no. 3, 319–35.

Stoer, Stephen R., and Fernanda Rodrigues (with the collaboration of Helena Barbieri) (2000). "Territórios Educativos de Intervenção Prioritária: Análise do Contributo das Parcerias," in Ana Maria Bettencourt, et al., *Territórios Educativos de Intervenção Prioritária.* Lisbon: Instituto de Inovação Educacional, 171–94.

Stoer, Stephen R., David Rodrigues, and António M. Magalhães (2003). *Theories of Social Exclusion.* Frankfurt am Main: Peter Lang.

6

Educational Policies and the Sense of Possibility

A Contribution to Democratic Education in a Progressive Age

António Teodoro

> *When I think about history I think about possibility—that history is the time and space of possibility. . . . In making history we choose and realize possibilities. And in making history we begin to be made by history.*
>
> —Paulo Freire (1989)

Born of the confluence of the illuminist project and that of the affirmation and construction of the nation-state with capitalism as a mode of organizing production, school systems have represented one of the central sites of the construction of modernity. In spite of the multiple practical difficulties and different rhythms of expansion, education quickly asserted itself as a global phenomenon that developed isomorphically in the modern world.

Throughout the nineteenth and twentieth centuries, first in Europe and later in other worldly spaces, school was transformed into a central element of linguistic and cultural homogenization, of national citizenship invention, of nation-state affirmation. As the authors who profile the perspective of the modern world system constantly remind us, the expansion of education is intimately linked to the construction of an indispensable reality of the new capitalist world economy, the *nation-state*: "Mass schooling becomes the central set of activities through which the central links between individuals and nation-states are forged" (Ramirez and Ventresca, 1992, 49–50).

This lengthy process implies the progressive expansion of schooling at all levels and for all social groups—and is as much of an outcome of the historical necessity of the new state of the capitalist world economy as of the powerful social struggles for school access, even though it is a public benefit to which all members of the community should have equal access.

The development of school for everyone—*mass schooling*, in Anglo-Saxon terminology—especially after World War II, was based on concretizing, in a limited way, the social-democratic ideal of equal opportunity. The central objective of public policy became the construction of a school that would provide for all, independent of social, economic, and cultural conditions, and would allow opportunities for social, professional, and cultural *promotion.*

From this perspective, school was understood to be a privileged space of social integration and inclusion, even if, as demonstrated by educational sociology, many of its effects were not precisely these. Utilizing Habermas's categories, these policies proposed a very strong regulating principle while, at the same time, affirming in equal measure a liberating principle, heir to the illuminist project of the formation of a *new man.* The concept of the *democratization of instruction* and the public policies associated with it, accurately represent this consensus, which dominated public and political discourse until the end of the 1970s.

However, the last two decades of the twentieth century witnessed the slow but steady affirmation of a new, hegemonic social bloc that has succeeded in imposing a new common sense of educational public policy, reducing democratic concepts to consumer practices, citizenship to a possessive individualism, and equality to resentment and fear of "the other."

Michael W. Apple, who has dedicated the principal of his works to combating this kind of right-wing education, maintains that the center of the construction of this discourse is in the transference of "the true realm of freedom" to the market and not, as before, to democratic politics (Apple, 2000, xiii). Which, according to Apple, "is nothing less than the recurrent conflict between property rights and person rights that has been a central tension in our economy" (2000, 17).

The consequences of this transference at the center of political discourse are evident in the hegemonic agenda of the public policies of contemporary education: on the one hand, in a clear association between diminished public investment and the privatization of important areas of public services and, on the other, in strong state regulations. It is, as Apple observes (2000, xxv–xxvii), "an odd combination of an emphasis on markets and 'choice' (weak state) on the one hand and an increasingly interventionist regulatory framework (strong state) that focuses on national curricula, national standards, and national testing on the other."

Moreover, a primary consequence of the *fear of the other*—here understood as much in the social as in the cultural realm—is the materialization of new forms of exclusion, for instance, in the systematic preoccupation with transforming all the evaluative processes into *rankings,* or in the return to the ideals of the meritocracy which has erased all the contributions that social science, particularly educational sociology, made in the last few decades toward understanding the processes of social and cultural reproduction.

Beginning with a rigorous analysis of the North American context, Apple believes that this new hegemonic social bloc is made up of an alliance of four main groups (e.g., Apple, 2000, 2001). The first of these, the *neoliberals*, represent the political and economic elite who intend to "modernize" the economy and the institutions that directly serve it. For this group, who are generally the leaders of this alliance, the "market" is the (only) solution for social problems, in accordance with their assumption that everything private is good and functions well and that everything public functions badly and is financially ruinous.

The second group, the *neoconservatives*, defend the return to high "standards of quality," to discipline, to the concern with "knowledge" and the selection of "the best" with which schools were associated before they opened their doors to the masses—all of this based on a somewhat nostalgic and romanticized vision of the past. This group has a particular preoccupation with curricula and pedagogical methods, blaming the *children of Rousseau* (and the educational sciences in general) for the poor "quality" of current schooling, resulting from a pedagogy centered on the interests of the student rather than on "the knowledge" of scientific disciplines. This group's main battles are focused on defining a central and basic curriculum and in strengthening teachers' "power to discipline."

The third group, the *authoritarian populists*, direct their main preoccupations toward the question of values like security, family, sexuality, and religious morality, which they consider to be put aside (or perverted) by the public schools. This group, particularly prevalent in the United States, strongly distrusts the state, is intensely community-minded, and has an ample political presence, normally through evangelical groups. Generally, they support the neoliberals and neoconservatives in their battles for *less state* and against the *secular humanism* that, in their view, is invading the public schools.

The fourth, and final, group is composed of an important fraction of the *new professional middle class*. According to Apple (2000, 2001), this group does not always agree with the agenda of the other groups, particularly on the ideological plane, since it generally takes more moderate and liberal positions. But, for reasons of profit, professional ideology, employment, and social mobility, this group is profoundly associated with the technical and gestational "solutions" of the educational dilemmas of this hegemonic agenda. *Accountability*, *efficiency*, and *management* comprise the competencies that form this group's own cultural capital and which it places at the service of the alliance that Apple categorizes as *rightist*.

The means that this rightist alliance possessed and utilized to construct its ideological and political hegemony are unquestionable because they are so integrated in this global process we call *neoliberal globalization*. But, rather than attempting to render it relative, the left has actually facilitated its ascension—for some, by relegating the core values of leftist thinking to secondary status so that they are nothing more than the French Revolutionary triptych [liberty, equality, fraternity]; for others, by featuring a discourse that though critically rigorous, is difficult, lacking a sense of possibility and real, concrete alternatives. Referring to this second field, where many intellectuals and critical educators are situated, Apple emphasizes: "I think that much of the discourse in which we participated was truly negative criticism. Negative work is important of course as a form of 'bearing witness' to oppression, but often it did not leave people with a sense of possibility" (2000, 166).

But, in this chapter, the central question that I want to formulate and for which I will seek to give a primary (and provisional) response is the following: Is it possible for the left, at the present time, to construct the bases of a new common sense capable of helping to formulate the educational agenda of a new social bloc interested in advancing (and realizing) progressive policies of peace, social justice, happiness, and freedom?

AN ALTERNATIVE EDUCATIONAL AGENDA

Very provisionally, there may be three starting points for this construction of an educational agenda capable of generating new, mobilizing common senses of hope and transformational human action. The first point, particularly important in the formation of those included in First World societies and among the privileged of the Third World, is expressed by the conviction that *we are all citizens of the same world* and that the struggle for happiness, well-being, and security of some is intimately linked to combating hunger, poverty, and the causes of injustice and social exclusion, at the level of both national societies and international relations. This implies seeking solutions and proposals not in a narrow national framework but in one that can be called *cosmopolitan globalization*, in the sense that Boaventura de Sousa Santos attributes to it:

It is about the organization of transnational resistance of the Nation-States, regions, classes or groups victimized by the unequal exchanges on which the globalized localisms and localized globalisms feed, using to their benefit the possibilities of transnational interaction created by the world system in transition, including those which result from the revolution in information and communication technologies. The resistance consists of transforming unequal exchanges into exchanges of shared authority which are translated into struggles against exclusion, subaltern inclusion, dependency, disintegration, demotion. (2001, 72–73)

The second starting point may represent the antidote to the *fear of the other* on which many of the policies of the current hegemonic agenda are based. Still following Santos's thinking, this antidote concerns materializing inter/multicultural policies in which the principle of equality is placed on par with the principle of the recognition of difference: *we have the right to be equal when difference makes us inferior; we have the right to be different when equality takes away our character.* Materializing this principle in politics and in pedagogical practice probably means seeking a happy synthesis between the principle of "equal opportunity," which dominated the social-democratic educational policies of the post–World War II period, and that of intercultural dialogue, that is, dialogue not just among different kinds of knowledge but among universes of different meanings, to some extent incommensurable.

The third starting point can be expressed in the attempt to materialize the motto *excellent schools for everyone*, understood as a reply (and an alternative) to the critique of the neoconservatives regarding the decline in quality of instruction and pedagogy of current schooling. António Magalhães and Stephen R. Stoer (2002, 2003) think about encountering this alternative while constructing a heuristic *continuum* between pedagogy and performance, remembering that if pedagogy without performance is "nothing," as the most radical neo-"meritocrats" maintain, there is also no performance without pedagogy for, no matter how mechanical the knowledge, it is always motivated, or rather mediated, by a pedagogical process.

> Thus, the assumption of the *continuum* not only permits one to map out the proposals of the different participants in the debate, it also suggests that, in the present context of a labor market structured by flexible capitalism, it is not compulsory that one remain confined to the radically pedagogical defense of education (as if pedagogical autonomy were independent with relation to the economy) nor to the reduction of education to performance (as if performance could exist without pedagogy). Alternative paths may be found in the differences (eventually incommensurable) that structure the educational mandates and in their mutually critical analysis. (Magalhães and Stoer, 2003, 50–51)

Conservative modernization is in the act of radically remodeling societal common sense as far as the educational agenda is concerned. The right obtained this hegemony because it succeeded in creating a decentralized unit in which each group sacrificed part of its individual project to enter into the areas that bind them all together (Apple, 2001). Can the left build a *tensile alliance* that, through systematic and persistent efforts, reconstructs another hegemonic common sense that can bring the emancipative dimensions of the educational process back to a primary place?

THE CONSTRUCTION OF A NEW TENSILE ALLIANCE

To determine the possible starting points for the elaboration of an alternative educational agenda to that of the right is unquestionably significant and important. But, at the same time, it is equally important for the political action to proceed from an effort of signification by the social and professional groups able to profit from (and construct) this other agenda, which will become the center of leftist governance.

A primary social group capable of integrating this tensile alliance may be designated—though perhaps in a less rigorous way than the sociologists would like—by the *lower middle class*, that is, by those social strata emerging into public life that (still) value education as a process of social ascension and of access to qualified employment and a superior social status for their children. These social strata generally evince preoccupations about access to education and about the quality of schooling their children receive, and about how all of this will manifest in the job market. "Everyone's school" must respond to the same demands for quality as when it was just for some.

A second group may be represented by the social movements that represent laborers and fight against new (and old) kinds of social exclusion. The old social movements are located here, of which the most relevant and influential is certainly the trade union movement, but also the peasant movements and even the new social movements made up of national and international human rights organizations. These groups are those that defend the environment and the ecological equilibrium in solidarity with oppressed peoples and represent and affirm the cultural rights of ethnic minorities; of citizens who suffer from mental or physical defects; of feminist movements and those which defend the right to sexual choice; of local development groups; literary movements; and artistic and cultural alternatives which struggle against the *unilateral thinking* and hegemonic forms of the so-called global culture. In this heterogeneous and plural group there nevertheless exists a common concern in the sphere of education: to resurrect the possible (and desirable) role of the school (and of life) as a site of *conscience* and *consciousness*—utilizing Paulo Freire's concept as one of the authors of reference for the league of organizations and movements which make up this group—which values processes and ways of behaving, *pedagogy*.

The third group may be composed of professional educators and scientists, particularly professors, educators, and researchers, who today constitute the most numerous group of intellectual laborers on our blue planet Earth and who, in many countries, enjoy high social prestige and have a strong and organized capacity for intervention on the social and political planes. Historically and as part of their social mission, professors and educators have played a leading democratic role in matters of educational access and power relations within schools, universities, and educational systems. The central political concern of the social mobilization of this group of professionals will possibly be the extent to which they join the struggle—the struggle for better conditions of life, work, and training that have been strongly degraded in the majority of the planet—in a political project that sees education and science as among the most important factors of individual and community empowerment.

The fourth group, particularly decisive in the democratic societies of the central countries and even of those on the semi-periphery of the world system, because of its electoral and media clout, can be called the *new middle class*. This group, characterized by the sociologist Basil Bernstein as the social class that seeks its sources of profit and social power in the cultural and scholastic capital it possesses (see Power and Whitty's article of synthesis, 2002), has come to assume a determining influence in the public agenda of education since the last third of the twentieth century and at least an important fraction of it, as Apple demonstrates (2001), has participated in the conservative alliance. To win this social group over to leftist politics implies a serious need to articulate the "school for all" as a place of academic excellence, in other words, to know how (or be able) to develop parallel policies on two decisive fronts—one that deals with the resolution of matters of access to and success in school on behalf of the least favored social and cultural groups, and another that deals with the quality and relevance of school trajectories, namely in the secondary and superior levels, with particular sensitivity to this group.

The construction of a tensile alliance on the social and political planes, which will allow the left to value what identifies it more than what divides it—a condition for the affirmation of new kinds of common sense that provide an alternative to those that the right succeeded in making part of its hegemony—implies overcoming what I see as deep traumas and mutual distrust among some of the left's principal components. The first trauma has to do with the strong neoliberal taint of the programs and, moreover, the governing practices of the socialist and social-democratic parties. The second necessitates that the (post)communists and leftist radicals overcome the Jacobinic concept of the state as the sole source of distribution and equality which mars most of their (in this case, less than Marxist) analyses.

Possibly, this tensile alliance will go through the exercise of constructing a program capable of establishing a dynamic synthesis between the reinforcement of *autonomy and individual responsibility*, modernity's still-unfinished proposition, and the affirmation of *community* as a central space not only in the construction of identities but also in the management of public affairs with *state reform*, bringing it nearer to the citizens so that political actions become transparent incentives for popular participation and democratic public spaces.

Contemporaneous societies are undergoing a period of profound change— of *bifurcation,* in the expression of Prigogine and Stengers (1986)—where *national space-time* has, little by little, lost primacy since the 1970s to the growing importance of *global and local space-times*, leading to a crisis of national *social contracts* which was the basis of the modern development of the central states as paradigms of the legitimacy of governance, economic and social well-being, security, and collective identity.

Thus it is important to rethink the *development project* that was central to the construction of modernity. Boaventura de Sousa Santos (1998) speaks of a *new social contract*, quite different from that of modernity, more inclusive, embracing "not only people and social groups, but nature itself" (46), which will, in his opinion, bring about a *democratic rediscovery of work*. In this last sense he is joined by Alain Touraine (1998), when the latter argues against the idea of *the end of work* and of its substitution by a *leisure society*, since what the last few decades have shown is the growing recession of a society of production and its domination by market society. In counterpoint to this vision, Touraine posits that we are about to enter a *civilization of work*, where the boundaries between work proper, games, and education are going to become progressively attenuated.

A new social contract also implies the transformation of the nation-state in what Santos (1998) calls the *newest social movement*. Such a proposition begins with the discovery that the sovereignty of the national state and its regulatory capabilities is eroding since it assumes that power is exercised "by networking in a vast and conflictive political field," through "a concatenation of organizations and flows," where "the coordination of the State functions as an imaginary center" (Santos, 1998, 66). In considering that this new political organization *has no center*, Santos then defends the *articulator-state*— whose institutionalization, he adds, has yet to be invented—which, as the very latest social movement, stimulates experimentation with alternative institutional designs that are not confined to representative democracy and confirm what he classifies as *redistributive democracy*. The new *welfare state*, he concludes, "is an experimental State and it is continual experimentation with the active participation of the citizens that guarantees the sustainability of its well-being" (67).

If this *new social contract* calls for a redefinition of the role of the state (and of theories about it), it also calls for the substitution of the model of a *contract*. Habermas (1997) posits that the source of legitimacy of modern juridical orders can only be found in the idea of *self-determination*: "the citizens must conceive of themselves, from moment to moment, as the authors of the laws to which they are submissive as designees" (479). According to Habermas, this means that the *model of discussion* or of *deliberation* will eventually supplant that of the contract—*the juridical community is not formed by a social contract, but rather by virtue of an agreement established by means of discussion.*

If we are going to accept the state's transformation into a field of *institutional experimentation*, we can also accept that the educational public policies of *leftist governance* must envision the school as a public space able to endow future (and current) generations with new ways of thinking about the construction of a more just world. A world, in Paulo Freire's symbolic expression, "rounder, less angular, more human, and in which preparations are being made for the materialization of the great Utopia: *Unity in Diversity*" (1993, 36).

To win (and transform) the state it is necessary to win (and transform) society, as Gramsci reminds us. And, in education, the great challenge for all those who identify with the patrimony of leftist values—liberty, equality, social justice, peace—is that of rebuilding a new common sense able to give daily support to a *pedagogy of hope* in the future of humanity, valuing political action as a space and time of possibility.

NOTE

Translation from Portuguese by Peter Lownds, Los Angeles, 25 June 2003.

REFERENCES

Apple, M. W. (2000). *Official Knowledge: Democratic Education in a Conservative Age*, 2nd edition. New York: Routledge.
———. (2001). *Educating the "Right" Way: Markets, Standards, God and Inequality*. New York: Routledge.
Freire, P. (1993). *Política e Educação*. São Paulo: Cortez.
Habermas, J. (1997). *Droit et démocratie: Entre faits et norms*. Paris: Gallimard.
Magalhães, A.M., and Stoer, S.R. (2002). A nova classe média e a reconfiguração do mandato endereçado ao sistema educativo. *Educação, Sociedade & Culturas* 18, 25–40.

————. (2003). Performance, Citizenship and the Knowledge Society: A New Mandate for European Education Policy. *Globalisation, Societies and Education* 1, no. 1, 41–66.

Power, S., and Whitty, G. (2002). Bernstein and the Middle Class. *British Journal of Sociology of Education* 4, no. 23, 595–606.

Prigogine, I., and Stengers, I. (1986). *La nouvelle alliance. Métamorphose de la science*, 2nd edition. Paris: Gallimard.

Ramirez, F. O., and Ventresca, M. J. (1992). "Building the Institution of Mass Schooling: Isomorphism in the Modern World." In *The Political Construction of Education: The State, School Expansion, and Economic Change*, ed. B. Fuller and R. Rubinson (pp. 47–59). New York: Praeger.

Santos, B. de S. (1998). *Reinventar a Democracia*. Lisbon: Gradiva/Fundação Mário Soares.

————. (2001). Os processos de globalização. In B. de S. Santos (org.), *Globalização: Fatalidade ou Utopia?* (pp. 31–106). Oporto: Afrontamento.

————. (2003). Por uma concepção multicultural dos direitos humanos. In B. de S. Santos (org.). *Reconhecer para libertar: Os caminhos do cosmopolitismo multicultural* (pp. 427–61). Rio de Janeiro: Civilização Brasileira.

Touraine, A. (1998). "Nous entrons dans une civilisation du travail," Paper presented to XIV World Congress of Sociology, Montréal, 26 July–1 August.

7

Rescuing Education from Corporate Takeover

From "Public Choice" to Public Action

Clementina Marques Cardoso

[T]ransformations are nothing more than all of us, all the social scientists and all non social scientists of this world transforming ourselves.

—Santos, 1994: 20

Transformation is a productive notion insofar it allows for the conceptualization of change beyond the narrow confines of isolated stages of development. Conceptualizing change as transformation requires taking into account existing layered practices and effects and renewed forms of control and resistance. These give origin to (re)new(ed) institutional arrangements and practices within the state and to "overlapping states." The concepts of "layered" (practices and effects) and "overlapping" (states) are extracted from the analysis of the Portuguese state developed by Santos (1993), proposing that we look at the state as a "geological composition with several layers, with different sedimentation, some old other recent, each with its own logic and strategic orientation" (41). The notion of overlapping states is a useful tool, which allows moving beyond the explanation of change over time to understand current features of the state and current underlying trends likely to influence the governance of education, pupils' learning, and professionals' teaching experiences. Let's take the case, for example, of the World Trade Organization's Council for Trade in Services having identified countries which expressed a "commitment to reduce trade barriers in education services" (Heyneman, 1999: 9) and the case of

barriers to free trade [in educational goods] [having] recently caught the attention of the U.S. Department of Commerce as well as other trade ministries. Among the principal concerns:

- monopolization of educational goods and services by public agencies
- closed systems of educational accreditation and professional licensure
- copyright infringement of educational brand names and protected items
- significant difference in tariffs on educational goods. (Heyneman, 1999: 9)

Or the case of global companies engaged in helping "educational clients expand into international markets, acquire new partners, provide public and private education and training services [. . .] and restructure and retrain workforces" (Heyneman, n.d.). What are the implications of governments facilitating such trend in the provision and governance of education? Because, as noted by Harvey, "to make the contemporary wave of neo-liberalism work, the state has to penetrate even more deeply into certain segments of political-economic life and become in some ways even more interventionist than before" (2000: 65). But most importantly, and because we make use of the notion *layered transformation*, we should also be asking what are the existing past and current resistances to obstructions to local democracy and social justice such as those mentioned above which can be mobilized?

This chapter attempts to do two things. First, drawing on my empirical research conducted in the mid 1990s and on my analysis developed thereafter, it offers an explanation to the nature of layered practices and effects in Portugal and England. It does this (1) by illustrating how the continuity of similar core areas of tension with the divisions of earlier periods was sustained or maintained to resurface at a later stage and (2) by drawing on Santos's notion of *parallel state* (1993) to elaborate on the notion of state as a multifaceted actor perfecting mechanisms of control and "enabling" autonomy. Second, departing from a typology of current changes, it explores what might be areas of emancipation from—but also resistance presented by—the colonization of social relations and public institutions by economic relations and private notions of contract and exchange, as well as conservative moral and religious codes.

The reconstitution of the state relies on reforms which, as I argued (2001: 14), penetrate accumulated layers shaping the national politics of education. These reforms rework and are reworked through new holders and forms of power. They are also sustained within a new political order that is embedded in new forms of "social and political regulation" (Harvey, 1989: 121). If changes are enshrined in national political and social divisions (Marques Cardoso, 2001: 17) and if transformation establishes continuities with the past to shape forms of control it must also establish continuities with past forms of resistance to tight control and be permeable to forms of local liberation in the name of participatory democracy and social justice. Identifying these continuities became more than ever necessary to ". . . discover the material, economic and above all organizational means to incite all competent researchers

[. . .] to collective discussion [. . .] and the creation of proposals [. . .] [for] a project of society" (f.t. Bordieu, 2001: xii–xiii).

Popkewitz reminded us that "the changes that we now witness in the school arena are changes that involve uneven movements of a long duration in multiple arenas" (1996: 47–48). Harvey advised that "the first difficulty is to encapsulate the nature of the changes we are looking at" (1989: 173). [Also that it] "behooves us to establish how deep and fundamental the change might be (121); [a] sea-change in the surface appearance . . . a transitional moment of grumbling crisis . . . solid transformation or temporary fix?" (188). Finally, Sousa Santos lead us to consider how "transformations are nothing more than all of us, all the social scientists and all non social scientists of this world transforming ourselves" (1994: 20).

The changes that we have been witnessing in education in the last two decades are of a double nature: changes brought about by the transformation in the wider political economy and changes introduced by education policy aimed at changing the foundations on which the provision, financing, management, and evaluation of schooling rest. Despite the varying forms these changes took and the degree of their effects, they were initiated by governments emphasizing the "improvement" of the "quality" of public services and of "professional standards" and the need for "lay participation" in public governance in their discourse on social reform. The management and governance of social institutions were regarded by governments as strategic areas of reform (Marques Cardoso, 2001) and governments have been playing a central role in facilitating these changes. Following the creed proposing "rolling back" the state, governments have been intensifying the presence of the hand of state institutions. This development presents both problems and possibilities for action. It is possible to have the public sphere, in many cases protected by constitutional guarantees, acting at various levels simultaneously. It can act to regulate the adverse effects of market regulation of social life; to roll back market-like mechanisms in public provision and financing of public services; and, finally, it can claim the moral right to obstruct practices initiated both by state institutions and by individual parents. While exercising their individual rights, parents might, in turn, obstruct social justice from being both the central concern of educational reform and the outcome of any public intervention. Public services are to be reclaimed as the guarantee for social justice. The guaranteed of private rights stops where it infringes the social right (all have) to education. The question remains. How can social justice be guaranteed in societies, cities, or other spaces that are segregated along the lines of use of land and resources which allow for enjoyment of what still only a minority can have? Analysis and reform strategies have all to answer this question.

During the last two decades, *improvement*, *quality*, and *participation* were the visible side of a return to conservative liberal principles in national governance that emerged in opposition to the existing broad political consensus on governance and management. The notions of (teaching) "quality," (professional and school) "autonomy," (parental) "participation" and (education) "standards" were redefined as governments lead and facilitated the process of creating new forms of government, civil society, community, state, citizenship, and social welfare. This return transformed the mandate for public schooling and the conditions for its provision, supply, and evaluation radically. Governments and the institutions of the state remained at the center of the transformations. These transformations changed both education and the social role of the state in relation to the autonomy of private individuals, institutions, and market institutions. The involvement of private economic agents in the supply, provision, and evaluation of education is growing. This involvement has been facilitated and promoted by governments on both the right and the left of the political spectrum—and this has been occurring in countries with strong, globally dominant economies and weaker, globally dominated economies.

Changes to the mandate of education cannot be isolated from the transformation of the social role of the state. Therefore, the analysis of education cannot be insulated from wider sociological analysis of current transformations. In fact, failing to incorporate wider analysis reflects analytical exercises, which lack the rigor sociological analysis has been building upon as a social science. Both the transformation and the action of policy have been captured by economic and political liberalism. The state has not been subjected to linear reductions or increases in its role. The state has been subjected to changes that are contradictory and paradoxical. Explaining these remains the challenge. Arguing on whether current forms of provision, supply, and financing of education provide more or less degrees of choice or autonomy is meaningless, unless we take into account the analysis of the role of these changes in social segregation and in the allocation of privileges.

Some social scientists with a concern for education have engaged in the analysis of current changes critically, creatively, and imaginatively. Others have engaged in an exercise of evaluation of the specific goals that the governments' changes were promised to achieve. At the same time the engagement—with the tendencies manifested by mainstream public opinion—presented itself as a challenge to all of us, policy, public opinion (generally manifested by social and political vested interests), and social analysis became entangled in "scientific" exercises with insufficient critical analysis. Common sense concepts and proposals for reform have not been sufficiently and radically challenged or—coupled with policy alternatives that challenge current social segregation in the offer—provision, financing of, and demand for education. Unveiling the transformation is not sufficient. There is a need for explanation. On the other hand, critical analysis has sometimes suffered from confinement to supportive quarters or strictly specialized forums.

Despite the fact that the introduction of policies informed by conservative political and economic liberalism occurred amidst political confrontations and social divisions reviving the grand themes, which were prominent during the transition from nineteenth century schooling, the new parameters of change have not always been critically analyzed. Instead, in some cases they have been accepted almost as a "natural" developmental stage that, as such, follows a period of crisis and brings a "new world." In some instances, pressure exercised by public opinion has been accepted as being the "truth" because, in theses narratives, we are made to believe that they are the expression of popular will. They are not and there is a need to analyze whose public opinion is being expressed and whose values and interests are being put forward. Accepting that the changes that we are now witnessing are a natural progression toward the achievement of such a "new" world, and limiting analysis to the evaluation of the goals this "new" world is supposed to provide, are traps that obstruct critical analysis.

There is evidence from various countries that new kinds of involvement of the private sector (companies, charities, families) in the regulation of public provision of schooling and maintenance of private provision of education interface with, first, "strong social polarization of schools," "an important educational segregation," and the growth in the number of families "choosing the best quoted private schools" (Barthon et al., 2003), as in the case of Northern France; second, the formation of a "hierarchy of schools" (Delvaux and Joseph, 2003) as is the case in Belgique francophone and in England (Marques Cardoso et al., 2003); and third, the trend in families escaping from "problematic schools" (Barroso and Viseu, 2003). As is the case in Portugal, quasi-market-type strategies are dwarfed by the ethic and provision of universal public education, which in turn is under threat by "government's recent guidelines . . . to promote a logic of the market" (Barroso and Viseu, 2003).

The conservative–liberal political and economic utopia does not pass the test of critical analysis. The political confrontations and social divisions that revived the above grand themes remind us how policymaking in education was conditioned by social segregation and academic selection up until the 1970s. But we seem to have forgotten those confrontations and, most importantly, the critique of limited democratization of access and participation which existed until then and which became confronted (and in a way colonized) by the neoliberal conservative critique of public schooling.

Taking account of past conflicts and social inequality and segregation when thinking of current transformations in the mandate, provision, management, financing, and official assessment of schooling, leads us to mobilize concepts, tools, and strategies to put the conservative liberal political and economic utopia to the test. It is in this way that transformation is a productive notion. Insofar as it allows for the conceptualization of change beyond the narrow confines of isolated stages of development, such a notion facilitates the analysis of current events both as a continuity with the past—so fiercely challenged up until the 1970s—and as containing the possibilities for both critical analysis and for the return to actions and to strategies capable of presenting a challenge to the conservative liberal political and economic utopia and the structure of political, economic, and social power(s) that sustain its foundations and the current state in many countries. Conceptualizing change as transformation requires taking into account existing layered practices and effects and renewed forms of control and resistance. These give origin to (re)new(ed) institutional arrangements and practices within the state and to *overlapping states*. Santos's analysis of the Portuguese state (1993), proposing that we look at the state as a "geological composition with several layers, with different sedimentation, some old other recent, each with its own logic and strategic orientation" (41), allows for the development of the concepts of *layered* (practices and effects) and *overlapping* (states). The notion of overlapping states is a useful tool, which allows moving beyond the explanation of change over time to understand current features of the state and current underlying trends likely to influence the governance of education, pupils' learning, and professionals' teaching experiences. In making use of the notion *layered transformation*, we should be asking: What are the existing past and current resistances and obstructions to local democracy and to social justice that can be mobilized by the new forms of involvement, by the various instances of the private sector and the older forms of private provision?

The challenge presented to social scientists engaged in the critical analysis of what is happening to the provision, management, financing, and assessment of schooling is not the production of legitimizing knowledge on whether the current conservative liberal political and economic utopia is delivering educational "choice" or "improvement" but rather understanding how the new forms of conservatism and liberalism are shaping the politics, institutions, and social relations by reference to a combination of principles that had been opposed in the past. The traditional opposition between the conservative and the liberal elite in power—which characterized the eight types of states, as defined by Rokkan and Lipset, in Europe (Colas, 1994: 509)—was broken. Not only did the 1980s reforms rework and were reworked through new holders and forms of power but they were also sustained within a new political order which was embedded in new forms of "social and political regulation" (Harvey, 1989: 121). Understanding this transformation remains the challenge and such understanding requires engaging in critical analysis of what, among others, the concepts of *choice, improvement, quality, participation, empowerment* proposed by the above utopia mean and, most importantly, determining what their current forms are as they shape the access to and participation in, not only, schooling but also employment. The double engagement in the understanding of concepts and the unveiling of the expression of policies in concrete spaces of action such as cities, neighborhoods, and educational institutions is the task that continues to be presented to us at the same time we understand these changes in a global dimension. This is because, at the same time the adoption of neoconservative liberal principles intersected nationally bound political and social divisions and models of democracy and social development resulting in national differences, a commonality among countries reflected the growing supremacy of individual parental rights of choice over the collective social right to education and the emergence of five tendencies:

- selection (of pupils by schools and of schools by parents);
- provision;
- financing;
- privatization; and
- management of teachers and teaching.

The convergence of national reforms incorporates a set of common developments that are deeply rooted in each nation. Despite membership of the European Union and the course of European policy harmonization in other policy areas, most triggers of changes mentioned above were not legislated at the European level. This was also in spite of educational training being one of "the two pillars . . . [where] there exists more of an intergovernmental type of cooperation" (Anderson and Eliassen, 1993: 22). At the same time the internationalization of conservative liberalism relied on the active commitment of governments, individual policymakers, and specific social and political groups and individuals in each country. Since the way in which reforms penetrated the existing (or created new) tensions and divisions was constrained by the national environment where these tensions developed, the impact of the introduction of market-oriented mechanisms and business-oriented procedures and systems in democratic institutions also varied according to the policy areas where they were introduced. The active role of national governments in spreading the conservative liberal policy framework does not reflect a straight reproduction of conservative liberal ideals. The "set of principles or theoretical model . . . [are not translated] into policy texts or practice in direct or pristine form. National policymaking is inevitably a process of bricolage" (Ball, 1998: 126) and of time-specific national compromises. The national forms that conservative liberalism takes are the product of the interaction between governments' active commitment or contribution to the international policy paradigm and the development of the national politics of education. The state has an active part in incorporating transformation, translating it into practice, and "to make the contemporary wave of neo-liberalism work, the state has to penetrate even more deeply into certain segments of political-economic life and become in some ways even more interventionist than before" (Harvey, 2000: 65). But it is also within the state that most tensions and conflicts are played out. Therefore, the resulting form of state is one that incorporates the movement generated by these processes where the national dictates and is dictated by what the international dimension of change takes. This is not a simple straightforward process as I have argued in the past (2001) because the conservative liberal movement is not a monolith. There are divisions within the conservative liberal movement and within governments, which shape institutional cultures and systems of management, governance, financing, admissions, inspection and which are specific to the blending of liberalism and conservatism. Governments' internal disputes over liberalism and between conservatism and liberalism influence forms and versions of decentralization, autonomy, and participation for example. These versions vary according to national traditions of conservatism and liberalism and to the type of institutional relations (past and present) existing between countries. Liberalism is a "controversial concept [of which the] meaning has shifted historically" (Held, 1998: 74). Liberalism is also characterized by a "vast internal variety and complexity" and "has acquired a different flavour in each of the different national cultures" (Gray, 1995: xii). This must be taken into account in order to, in turn, take into account that various sets of principles and regulatory models influence the notion and goals of, for example decentralization or privatization, governments' programs, and, consequently, the process of policy formulation and implementation. Each set will propose different versions of autonomy and of civil society on which the notions of decentralization or privatization depend. This multiplicity of meanings and mandates shape, in turn, the notions of local development, community, local freedom to participate in decision making, delegation, participation, and autonomy. The meaning and purpose of complementary objectives such as diversity, quality, efficiency, assessment/evaluation and choice, are also influenced by this multiplicity.

Nationally, internal tensions arise from the "internal variety" of liberalism, the divisions within conservative liberalism and from national histories while the opposition to social forms of democracy, education, freedoms, and rights remain consistent because neoconservative liberalism is not a loose aggregate of ideas.

> [Despite] diversity . . . , political manifestations and social ramifications . . . [of] the ideas comprising radical right ideology [that] are complex, multifaceted and even internally inconsistent . . . , [are strongly locked on the] three ideological themes of economic individualism, cultural traditionalism and authoritarian populism. (Midgley, 1991: 3, 8)

The converging form conservative liberalism has been taking in the past two decades is grounded on a narrow version of democracy and implies a continuity with past shortcomings on democratization. Individual freedom is to be pursued without public guarantees for social rights. Education is to be accessed by exercising rational, individual, calculated choice. Economic freedom is to be pursued with limited economic justice. There is a tendency to "downgrade or deny the validity of social rights and positive freedoms and insist instead that legal and political rights are fundamental" (Glennerster, 1991: 173). The "free" market principle confines social rights. Education acquires a market value. The notion that educating children is an economic investment is emphasized to highlight the need for its provision to be subjected to rational individual choice. Individual choice is to maximize educational, cultural, and financial capital. Thus, as in a private business, investment requires capital and expertise. The notions of unequal value, unequal benefits, and social distinction are not integrated in the version of (market) diversity. "Optimal" individual behavior and economic efficiency replace the requirements of social equality. The norms of competition overshadow democratic requirements and replace redistribution criteria with economic efficiency. Unequal market relations and market-produced outcomes—which in effect had previously been reduced by redistributive policies—are not taken into account as being an obstacle to the foundation of democratic rights. Competition becomes the basis for the new form of allocation of services where one individual is to gain what another individual is to lose. In many cases, the Darwinian principle of natural selection is transferred to social selection: only the fittest survive educational assessments. Changes in schools follow narrow definitions of *improvement* based on the oppositions between good/bad, efficient/inefficient, or useful/useless.

　　The corporate takeover of education is not a process of direct acquisition of the public sector. The form that privatization of the public space, institutions, practices, and educational mandates takes is a process of slow, persistent, cumulative, almost invisible change. It takes the hearts of the public, of professionals, and of the managing class; it creeps between existing sets of relations and amongst practices until it lodges itself in a comfortable position from which it will be hard to be removed. Understanding the process by which it embeds itself within existing systems, states, and sets of relations is as urgent as understanding the way by which it is imposed and explicitly forced through so analysis is no longer overtaken by policy. And so analysis does not follow behind policy events. This involves being alert also to the way in which transnational[1] organizations—but also regional organizations such as the European Union—facilitate or obstruct changes. There are indications that

> in recent years, this Europeanization [of commercial lobbying] trend has been strengthened by the European Commission rewarding those firms that developed regular European representation with favored access to it's policy forums. . . . We are observing the establishment of a European public policy system that, through its restricted European actor 'entry' requirements, can influence domestic actors' use of national public policy systems and create new political business alliances at the European level. . . . The large firm, in its quest for improved access to the European public policy system, has become a partner and agent of European integration and a mechanism for institutional change. (Coen, 1998: 98)

The transformation taking place is both accepted and resisted by various groups (or within one same group) but its success relies first on installing certain conditions. Some of these are the definition of *universal schooling* in terms of an educational minimum where school access and educational success are guarantees for social rights, and are placed in opposition to the individual's right to preferential access. The liberal conception of rights, where rights are conceived as being opposed to each other, comes to override the "integrated" (Canotilho and Moreira, 1991: 44) version of rights. The negative individual right of noninterference with the freedom to learn is placed in opposition to the positive right of all to education. The collective social rights which are a guarantee for the exercise of individual freedom of education become isolated and their content is emptied. This way, the state's guarantee of this individual freedom is to be taken over by private (family) investors in education. Consumer choice is to replace social (sometimes constitutional) guarantees. Educational markets are to become the private arena where individuals exercise choice and (civil society) institutions influence financing, resources allocation, surveillance, and decision making. Enforcement of the right to education is, as in other private markets, to be left to the private and only ultimately (via private litigation) to the public sphere.

As in other markets, private enforcement will be unequally exercised. The politics of education are, in this way, also transferred from the public to the private arena. The market is to regulate liberty and freedom, leaving rights outside the framework of the state's privatized system of allocation, financing, and provision of public schooling. The public management of private tax income by government is targeted by neoliberals as being at the root of problems in education. The private concentration of revenue is removed from government's concerns. The private market economy plus private civil society (with minimal welfare to keep social order) is preferred to the private market economy plus welfare state formula in public policymaking. A new mixed economy is forged. The establishment of educational markets reduced the role of planning the use of private revenue and transformed the system of 'relocation of enterprises and household income taxes' (Glennerster 1997: 11). Democratic control—which conservative liberals oppose—is reduced. Without reducing central government's intervention in schooling, neoconservative liberal reforms reduce democratic influence. As at the end of the nineteenth century, business freedom to trade (and to maximize profit) is extended to promote the individual's freedom to maximize private individual capital. Workers (taxpayers) are to become private (financial and educational) investors.

By standing in opposition to participatory democratic principles, institutional models, or practices but also to further democratization of educational participation, conservative liberal governance recreates old "grave doubts . . . [about] the possibility of realising [the] ideal of . . . democracy as the rule of the people by means of the maximum participation of all people" (Pateman, 1995: 2). As emphasized by Gray, "liberalism constitutes a single tradition, rather than two or more traditions or a diffuse syndrome of ideas" (1995: xiii).

However, the corporate takeover of education is also reflected in more direct and obvious processes of change—as those described by Heyneman above in relation to the World Trade Organization's Council for Trade in Services. These processes are not going to disappear by waving a magic wand. Unveiling these processes through analysis which relies on simple causal explanations is not sufficient to provide alternatives for action and for analysis of the subtle nature in which these processes creep inside the public sphere—into the organization, management, financing, and evaluation of public institutions and public professional practices. Understanding the implications of governments facilitating the introduction of forms of privatization in the provision and governance of education requires a set of conditions but the analysis capable of mobilizing forms of local liberation in the name of participatory democracy and social justice faces several important obstacles. Harvey alerted us for the fact that, "to the degree that we are witnessing a historical transition, still far from complete and . . . bound to be partial in certain important respects, so we have encountered a series of theoretical dilemmas"

(1989: 173). These are complemented by specific difficulties. The first is perhaps the tendency to reproduce analytical models and concepts produced from within economics and in that way colonize and debilitate sociological analysis. Analysis may also suffer from being limited by constraints derived from what Santos defines as the *dominant scientific paradigm* (1991: 10):

> being a discipline-based knowledge, [modern science's] knowledge tends to be knowledge . . . that segregates the organisation of knowledge oriented to police the borders between disciplines and to repress those that want to transpose them. (1991: 46)

"This requires [parting], with some pain, with . . . [concepts and institutional practices to give birth to] an emerging paradigm" (Santos, 1991: 35) which is "non-dualistic . . . grounded in [the aim of] overcoming distinctions . . . such as nature/culture, natural/artificial, live/inanimate, mind/matter, observer/observed, collective/individual, animal/person [. . .], dichotomic distinctions" (39–40). It also requires embracing "methodological transgression [in order] not to follow a unidimensional, easily identifiable style [but rather] a configuration of styles [which incorporates] . . . the criteria and personal imagination of the scientist" (Santos, 1991: 49). "Only a constellation of methods can capture the silence which persists between each language that questions [reality]" (48).

The analysis of education policy has faced particular problems. The "politics of education [was] a relatively neglected field [while] the economics of education [had became] a very popular one" (Glennerster and Hoyle, 1972: 194). Also, the study of education was neglected in policy-oriented studies for a long period. Any present study of education policy is confronted with this legacy (Marques Cardoso, 1995: 8–11) but is also presented with the legacy left by the various approaches to the study of education, including educational studies, educational studies of policy, policy studies, and education politics. Only recently has there been a shift in approaches to the study of education policy (1995: 16). Such legacy was transferred to the field of comparative education. There has been a division between the emphasis on "socioeconomic transformation" and on "political institutions and political ideologies as key factors shaping outcomes" (Castles, 1998: 3) in cross-national comparative public policy. The irreconcilable opposition between studies focusing on policy areas and comprehensive cross-national comparisons (19) continues to exist. *Comparative public policy* is confined to the limits of the inherited use of economic and demographic indicators to explain the "differences in levels and changes in public policy outcomes" (4). The tradition of strong state control with weak intervention in public provision, the religious, communitarian, and family forms of social welfare (which are important features shaping public policy in those countries) and the politics of social policy are left out of international research. The new classification of "families of nations" (8) continues with the arbitrary association of countries based on having (in the case of Portugal, Spain, and Greece) "many affinities as part of the ancient Mediterranean cultural world [and] . . . the lateness of their economic, social and political modernisation" (8–9). Public spending–based studies continue to be at the center of controversy. On the one hand they are advocated in that they "reduce the problem [of allocating the benefits of specific expenses to specific groups] to the question of the percentage of total public spending that the social invoice represents seems to be justified. . . . That gives us a measure of the progress of the country in the direction of the Welfare State" (Esping-Andersen, 1993: 592).

On the other hand, such a "measure of progress" excludes education from analysis of changes to the social role of the state. The transformation which is taking place requires accounting for specific changes and processes by which these are achieved. Some of theses processes are (re)new(ed). Since at the core of the reconstitution of the state are accumulated layers of policy action and inaction and, as already mentioned new forms of "social and political regulation" (Harvey, 1989: 121) the study of policy convergence requires an approach which analyses reforms in the context of long-term social development. Such an approach must also take into account the continuity in both government and social regulation in general. We must attempt to become closer to analysis that "being total, is not deterministic, being local, is not descriptivist" (1991: 8).

There is a further difficulty. The United States initiated the dissemination of the belief that we are living in an age of crisis in schooling.[2] The Anglo-Saxon world also initiated a particular form of policy analysis which presents serious problems for the study of the transformations which are taking place in other countries. Although they are now being overcome by the presence of significant studies and analysis of both local and global changes originated in non-Anglo-Saxon countries, the long acknowledged language differences has imposed real constraints. In the Anglo-Saxon world, policy has been defined in a rather instrumental manner (see Ham and Hill, 1992). It has been identified as referring to a legislative text, a measure or group of measures, and procedures to be implemented (but also to their absence) in order to achieve a purpose in a system. The word *policy* does not have a direct translation into, for example, German, Portuguese, French, or Spanish. In Portuguese and French, the closest translation for *education policy* is *politica* and *politique* respectively. These, in turn, do not translate into the English language. *Policy* being, as far as we are concerned, a "course or principle of action adopted or proposed by a government, party, business or individual, etc." (The Concise Oxford Dictionary, 1991) and *politica* being "the science or art of governing a nation, the administrative direction a government takes, the organizing principles of government action" (Dicionario da Lingua Portuguesa, 1979)—then *politica* becomes *politics* in the English language. Wildavsky asserts that "it is more important to practice policy analysis then to spend time defining it . . . [because nothing] is more stultifying than a futile search for Aristotelian essences" (Ham and Hill, 1992: 4). However, what is meant by *policy* is a fundamental issue that needs consideration from the outset of any study (Marques Cardoso, 1995: 10–11). As noted by Hantrais and Ager in 1985, the "language and cultural barriers existing between the members of an international research team are [. . .] rarely discussed in any detail as a major issue likely to affect the outcome of the project. [. . .] [Language] is not simply a medium for conveying concepts, it is part of the conceptual system, reflecting institutions, thought processes, values and ideology" (Hantrais and Mangen, 1996: 7).

Ignoring those aspects does not only affect methodology but also the understanding of specific phenomena or issues from the outset.

THE NATURE OF LAYERED PRACTICES AND EFFECTS IN PORTUGAL AND ENGLAND

This section sketches[3] the divisions which preceded and were embedded in the formulation of changes to the governance and the management of education in Portugal and England until 1996. Political divisions had continuity with historical developments in social policy, as well as in the definition of mandates for schooling. Those divisions were visible in six areas[4] affected by reforms at the end of the 1980s and showed a continuity of similar core areas of tension with the divisions manifested in earlier periods. Curriculum, assessment, and teaching methods were the three areas where tension was more visible. In Portugal, the areas where parliamentary parties were most divided in 1986 were parental choice and public financing. Right-wing[5] parties argued that education provisions should be made taking into account resource scarcity. Also, they argued that the state should finance private education to guarantee parental choice and equal treatment of private and public education. Private education was associated with the claim that the families' right to control their children's education should be paramount. In addition, right-wing parties argued that compulsory education should not be provided on a comprehensive basis and that technical and vocational courses should be integrated in specialized secondary school programs. They also argued that professional training should be organized in partnership with businesses. In 1986, the discussion of the Education Bill in Parliament developed according to party political division on essential issues. This division reflected traditional political divisions between the support for a democratic state where participation and citizenship were based on individualism and on the free market as a social regulator and a democratic state where social citizenship and participative rights, as well as public planning according to need, were supported. The political divisions were similar to the ones that were observed during the discussion of the 1986 and 1988 English Education Bills. The divisions that developed between 1976 and 1986 in Portugal presented similarities with divisions that had developed in the post–World War II period in England. The political divisions that gained expression in 1986 were embedded in the attempt to restore what teachers' representatives saw as traditions that had been rejected in 1974 for being nondemocratic. Throughout the debate of the 1986 bill, the definition of a legislative framework—based on constitutional rights, on provision according to need, on equal opportunities in the access to education and equality in educational achievement, on participatory management and democratic participation in educational decision making—was systematically (but unsuccessfully) challenged. This challenge came from within political (party) projects influenced by principles which emphasized the need for a public commitment to maintain a private system of education, to make public provision dependent on available resources and to introduce notions of parental choice to the main body of the Education Act (see discussions on articles 1 and 2 in Sampaio, 1988: 31–33). The importance of private education and parental choice were emphasized by CDS. Financing was defined in general terms but it was a source of contention within PSD. All other parties advocated the need to guarantee public financing of schooling. The Act would guarantee that "education should be considered one of the national priorities to be included in the state's budget plan" (article 42, 1, of the Act); PSD proposed that article 42 should be abolished since financing should be left to be defined by governments. These were the terms under which, in PSD's 1987 Party manifesto and program for education, education financing was presented as a priority for reform. This program presented many constraints to the implementation of the 1986 principles of democratic participation in the management and governance of education and of participatory democracy. Parliamentary discussions were characterized by a high degree of conflict between, on the one hand, the growing influence of the neoliberal national agenda during the first part of the 1980s, the general strength of the international move toward neoconservative liberalism, and the demands of an increasingly deregulated European economy and, on the other hand, the national constitutional principles on social development and education.

As explained by FENPROF'S leader, there was great awareness of this split among both teachers' representatives and members of Parliament.

> The entry to the EEC also influenced the process . . . greater investment in human resources [was emphasised]. . . . For many, the idea was to go back to the (1973) Education Act (with democratic principles at its base). . . . We (the teachers' representatives) exerted pressure from the outside . . . and when it wasn't possible to reach positions close to the ones we already had, then, we thought we would need to maintain some ambiguity, to compromise but not let things appear so clear that [it would risk] our positions being defeated later. This was the case with teachers' training. . . . That was a strategy. (Interview on 30/3/1995)

The implementation of local government structures, which would allow for the creation of decentralized forms of management and governance, was put on hold until 1986. By then, the absence of a national reform and a twelve year history of running schools without the establishment of conditions for local democracy and participatory systems left the basis of collegiate school management very vulnerable to criticism. Criticism, which originated both from those wanting to see criteria for participatory democracy to be implemented and from those embracing public choice[6] critiques of public education and collegiate management. The Portuguese Parliament was not merely divided on the issue of parental participation in education. Local democracy was understood by the left and the majority of teachers as meaning the creation of structures for the local government of education. Professional autonomy was understood, within the context of the need for government's commitment to value the teaching profession, to consolidate the democratic basis on which teaching would be exercised and to break away from a system where teaching was strongly regulated according to the needs of the pre-1974 authoritarian regime and the constraints of central administrative rule. This willingness to break away from the pre-1974 legacy is at the origin of article 45, 3, which subordinates administrative to educational criteria. This was a very sensitive issue, which led the CDS to oppose teachers. CDS proposed that number 3 of article 45 should be removed from the Act. Professional autonomy was viewed by teachers as being strongly tied to school management. Planning and governance would be shared between elected teachers-managers and local government. The advancement of this view was informed by the wish to move away from the legacy of a framework of governance, which had pushed teachers away from their initial commitment to being elected to participate in the governance and management of schools. Overall, the 1986 Act recognized the need to develop a national public education service which was freed from political authoritarianism and which recognized civil liberties, democratic freedom, and equal participation in national development. In this context, the management and governance of education and of schools had the mandate to implement direct participation and to promote equal access and educational achievement to every child. The Act contained both possibilities and constraints.

By the mid 1980s, the overlapping of various types of state was one of the specific characteristics of public management and governance in Portugal and this was different from England. As explained below, elements of the authoritarian regime met democratic reforms and practices and various versions of democracy informed the reforms of the public services in a very short period of time (Santos, 1993: 41 and 27).

In Portugal, the type and the nature of educational issues and battles fought from 1976 to 1986 were indicative of the nature of a future shift and were an important influence on the way policy was formulated in the second part of the 1980s. Unlike in England, where the shift in policy steered by neoconservative liberal governments transformed established national public systems, in Portugal, the transformation took place as national public systems were developing: "it was as if Portugal was going through a welfare state crisis without ever having had the welfare state" (Santos, 1993: 45). In the 1976 Constitutional socialist consensus, on the need to introduce public and social citizenship rights, education was politically defined as having an important role in achieving this. However, the 1976 Constitution never proposed the creation of a welfare state, as the aim of the Constitution was the creation of a socialist state not of a capitalist democracy (Santos, 1993: 44). By 1986, a political split about the role and the purpose of education was established within the existing broad consensus. The origins of the shift in policy are, as described below, different from the context of the changes that took place in the 1970s in England (Santos, 1993: 19 and 25). The political split that gained strength in Portugal began increasingly to resemble the conflict, tension, and changes which developed in England in the 1980s. In 1986, the British Conservative government initiated what would become the "first really large structural change to the education system since the 1944 Act" (Glennerster, 1995: 200). Parliament began by approving the no. 2 Education Act that would change the existing framework for school governance. The 1988 ERA established a new national education system and a new framework for the management of local government–maintained state schools. In 1993, the Schools Act changed the framework for the administration, management, and governance of newly created and centrally maintained state schools (grant-maintained schools). Changes to administration were embedded in changes to central/local government relations and defined, readjusted, and contested in the "reworking of the ideological terrain of ideological politics" (Ball, 1990:

8). Thus, by 1986, consensus on curriculum provision, teaching methods, management, and governance of schooling, as well as on educational social policy measures designed to address the issues of social inequality and social justice identified in the 1960s, had been left behind in England to give way to three new forms of control of the management and governance of schools: ministerial and central departmental control, quasi-governmental (Quango[7]) control, and nonprofessional (lay) control. In England, between the 1960s and the early 1980s, "social democratic management" (Grace, 1995: 34) developed based on notions and practices of "consultative management" and "shared decisionmaking" (38–39). The practice of management was, marked by what Grace described as "contradictions, limitations and vulnerabilities" (1995: 194). The essential problem of low democratization of public decisionmaking was real in both countries. The public choice critique of central government departments, of teachers, and of schools was successful in isolating educational management and local government as being causes of educational problems, which had long been the focus of the professional critique of public education. The British Conservative government exploited a critique that had been a strong asset of political opposition groups. The constraints to local autonomy had also been a problem that had been identified by teachers and by advocates of universal public systems of education in both countries. The political divisions existing in the two countries at the stage of policy formulation shaped the process of implementation.

The type of state resulting from these developments far from being a new replacement for an old state is a transformed state. It is a strong weakened state (Marques Cardoso, 2003). A state that is, at times and across initiatives, a strong central state with a weak local state, that is a strong central state with a strong local state, or that is a weak central state. Its forms vary according to the initiatives and partnerships across and between the public and private sectors. It is a centralized state, it is not a centralized state; it is a decentralized state, it is not a decentralized state. It is up to us to find out what forms it takes and what they do to teachers, families, and students. What they do to the students in particular can be seen in geographical spaces in local areas: where parents choose the schools they want their children to go to while other parents send their children to the school closest to home; where schools take the initiative to choose the students they want; where schools compete and collaborate with other schools; and where schools collaborate with private economic agents.

It is a state where several forms of regulation are exercised simultaneously:

• Market
• Central government

- Local government/private providers
- (Public and private) Contracting/bidding (Marques Cardoso et al., 2003)

It is a state with institutions which incorporate several decades of conflict, struggle, resistance, oppression of social freedoms and individual rights, and several layers of institutional practice and informal private (commercial, religious, and lay) influence and steering action. At the same time, this form of state also relies on stronger awareness of the workings of the political system and mechanisms of control by the wider population. These and new forms of social mobilization allow for the mobilization of resistance to tight control and for forms of local liberation waiting to be enacted in the name of participatory democracy and social justice. This, as Bourdieu reminded us, requires us to "discover the material, economic and above all organizational means to incite all competent researchers . . . to collective discussion . . . and the creation of proposals . . . [for] a project of society" (Bourdieu, 2001: xii–xiii).

This can be achieved by making use of, first, the notion of "parallel state" (Santos, 1993). This notion acts as a starting point to think about the state as a multifaceted actor that perfects mechanisms of control and of "facilitating" autonomy. This is an actor with a structure and a set of relations where the notions and the "solutions of the old paradigm coexist with the solutions of the new paradigm" (Santos, 1998: 66).

Second, if we develop a typology of current changes, we are able to explore what might be areas of emancipation from but also resistance presented by the colonization of social relations and public institutions by economic relations and private notions of contract and exchange, as well as conservative moral and religious codes. This will not only be a way of understanding the emerging form the state is taking but also of thinking about a state that, as proposed by Santos, is waiting to be invented (1998: 65). Understanding the forms the emerging and future state might take requires taking into account the existence of continuities and change, tensions and conflict—and this remains the most urgent task before us.

NOTES

1. Several OECD reports have been influencing national changes worldwide. Among there are: Performance Management in Government (OECD, Public Management Committee, 1996); Budgeting for Results, Perspectives on Public Expenditure Management (OECD 1995); Integrating People Management into Public Service Reform (OECD 1996); Support of Private Sector Development (OECD, Development Assistance Committee, 1995); Schools and Quality: An International Report (1989); School: A Matter of Choice and Quality in Teaching (1994); and Measuring the Quality of Schools and Schools under Scrutiny, (1995).

2. This was expressed in several reports: A Nation at Risk, (N.C.E.E., 1983); Educating Americans for the 21st Century (N.S.B., 1983); Carnegie Report on Secondary Education in America (1983); Paideia Proposal (1982); The Council of Chief State School Officers Report (1985); the National Science Foundation Report (1985); the National Science Board Work on Indicators (1991); Education Counts and a Trial State Assessment of the National Assessment of Educational Progress (1987); the Creation of an Indicator System by the Office of Educational Research and Improvement (1988); the National Education Goals Panel Report (1991); and the National Council on Education Standards and Testing (1992).

3. Detailed analysis and specific developments can be found in Marques Cardoso (2001: 67–93). See Marques Cardoso (2004) for analysis of the early impact of national reforms on schools.

4. The areas of central–local government relations, government–professional relations, local government–school relations, and educational expertise–policymaking relations; of institutional distribution of (management) authority and responsibilities; and, finally, of the relationship between professional autonomy and government control of the definition of priorities for schooling.

5. This division is kept to follow Sampaio (1988)'s analysis. The Social Democrat (Partido Social Democrata—PSD) and the Centre Democrat Social (Centro Democrata Social—CDS) parties were characterized as right-wing parties. Nevertheless, the adoption of this analysis does not imply the acceptance of a narrow definition of left- and right-wing political parties.

6. See Marques Cardoso (2003a) for a detailed analysis of the influence and presence of public choice critiques and models.

7. This stands for Quasi-Nongovernmental Organization.

REFERENCES

Andersen, S., and Eliassen, K. A. (1993). *Making Policy in Europe: The Europeification of National Policy Making*. London: Sage.

Ball, S. J. (1990). *Politics and Policy Making in Education: Explorations in Policy Sociology*. London: Routledge.

Ball, S. J. (1998). "Big Policies/Small World: An Introduction to International Perspectives in Education Policy," *Comparative Education* 34, no. 2: 119–30.

Barroso, J., and S. Viseu. (2003). "Local Area of Interdependence between Schools," *Reguleduc Report*. Lisbon: FPCE, UL.

Barthon, C., and B. Monfroy, with collaboration from L. Demailly, M. Tondellier, and J. Verdiere. (2003). "Les Espaces Locaux d'Interdependance entre College," *Reguleduc Report*. Lille: CLERSE/IFRESI.

Bordieu, P. (2001). *Contrafogos 2, Por um Movimento Social Europeu*. Oeiras: Celta Editora.

Canotilho, J. J., and V. Moreira. (1991). *Fundamentos da Constituicao*. Coimbra: Coimbra Editora.

Castles, F. G. (1998). *Comparative Public Policy—Patterns of Post-War Transformation*. Northampton, MA: Edward Elgar.

Coen, D. (1998). "The European Business Interest and the Nation-State: Large Firm Lobbying in the European Union and Member-States," *Journal of Public Policy* 18, no. 1: 75–100.

Colas, D. (1994). *Sociologie Politique*. Paris: Presses Universitaires de France.

Delvaux, B., and M. Joseph. (2003). Les Espaces Locaux d'Interdependance entre Colleges, *Reguleduc Report*. Louvain: CERISIS, UCL.

Esping-Andersen, G. (1993). "Orçamentos e democracia: o estado-providência em Espanha e Portugal, 1960–1986," *Análise Social* 28, no. 122, (3o): 589–606.

Gentili, P. (1998). "A complexidade do óbvio: a privatização e seus significados no campoeducacional." In *A Escola Cidadã no Contexto da Globalização*, ed. L. H. Silva. Petropolis: Ed. Vozes.

Glennerster, H. (1991). *Paying for Welfare: The 1990s*. London: Harvester Wheatsheaf.

Glennerster, H. (1995). *British Social Policy since 1945*. Oxford, UK: Blackwell.

Glennerster, H. (1997). *Paying for Welfare, 3rd ed.—Towards 2000*. London: Prentice Hall/Harvester Wheatsheaf.

Glennerster, H., and E. Hoyle. (1972). "Educational Research and Education Policy," *Journal of Social Policy* 1, no. 3: 193–212.

Grace, G. (1995). *School Leadership, beyond Educational Management: An Essay in Policy Scholarship*. London: The Falmer Press.

Gray, J. (1995). *Liberalism*. Buckingham, UK: Open University Press.

Ham, C., and M. Hill. (1992). *The Policy Process in the Modern Capitalist State*. London: Harvester Wheatsheaf.

Hantrais, L., and S. Mangen, eds. (1996). *Cross-National Research Methods in the Social Sciences*. London: Pinter.

Harvey, D. (1989). *The Condition of Post-Modernity*. Oxford, UK: Blackwell.

Harvey, D. (1996). *Justice, Nature and the Geography of Difference*. Oxford, UK: Blackwell.

Harvey, D. (2000). *Spaces of Hope*. Berkeley: University of California Press.

Held, D. (1998). *Models of Democracy*. Cambridge, MA: Polity Press.

Heyneman, S. (1999). The Growing International Market for Educational Goods and Services. Paper to Oxford Conference on Poverty, Power and Partnership. (9–13 September 1999), Oxford.

Heyneman, S. (n.d.). Biographical sketch provided by author.

Interview with Leader of the Federação Nacional de Professores (FENPROF). In Marques Cardoso, C. (2001). Decentralization, School Autonomy and the State in England and Portugal: 1986–1996. Unpublished Ph.D. thesis. London: LSE.

Marques Cardoso, C. (1995). Assumptions and Traditions in the Scientific Community: The Difficulties and Challenges of Comparing Education Policy in the European Union, Analyzed through the Study of Two Most Different Countries. Unpublished paper presented to the European Conference on Educational Research, University of Bath, September.

Marques Cardoso, C. (2003). "Do Público ao Privado: Gestão racional e critérios de mercado em Portugal e em Inglaterra." In *A Escola Pública: Regulação, desregulação, privatização*, ed. João Barroso. Porto: Edições Asa.

Marques Cardoso, C. (2004). "La Autonomia, los Mechanismos del Mercado y la Democracia Local: Los Colégios Educativos entre la Gobernanza Pública y Privada." In Revista de Educación, n° 333, Enero-Abril. Madrid, Ministerio de Educatión, Cultura y Deporte, pp. 59–90.

Marques Cardoso, C., S. J. Ball, C. Vincent, M. Thrupp, D. Reay, and S. Neath. (2003). Additive and Hyper Regulation in England: Making Sense of the Regulation of Secondary Education in the Inner City. Paper presented at the International Seminar of the Reseau d'Analyse Pluridisciplinaire des Politiques Educatives on Governance, Regulation and Equity in European Education Systems, 20–21 March, Institute of Education, University of London.

Marques Cardoso, C., S. J. Ball, C. Vincent, M. Thrupp, D. Reay, and S. Neath. (2004 work in progress). *Additive and Hyper Regulation in England.* Paper presented to the International Interdisciplinary Seminar of the Reseau d'Analyse Pluridisciplinaire des Politiques Educatives on Governance, Regulation and Equity in European Education Systems, 20–21 March 2003, Institute of Education, University of London.

Midgley, J. (1991). "The Radical Right, Politics, and Society." In *The Radical Right and the Welfare State: An International Assessment*, ed. H. Glennerster and J. Midgley. Hemel Hampstead, UK: Harvester Wheatsheaf.

Pateman, C. (1995). *Participation and Democratic Theory.* Oxford, UK: Cambridge University Press.

Popkewitz, T. S. (1996). "Rethinking Decentralisation and State/Civil Society Distinctions: The State as a Problematic of Governing," *Journal of Education Policy* 11, no. 1: 27–51.

Sampaio, J. S. (1988). *Posição dos Partidos Parlamentares perante a Lei de Bases do Sistema Educativo.* Lisbon: Cadernos Fenprof.

Santos, B. de S. (1990). *O Estado e a Sociedade em Portugal (1974–1988).* Porto: Edicões Afrontamento.

Santos, B. de S. (1990). "O estado e os modos de produção de poder social." In *A Sociologia e a Sociedade Portuguesa na Viragem do Século, Actas do I Congresso Português de Sociologia, Vol. II.* Lisbon: Editorial Fragmentos.

Santos, B. de S. (1991). *Um Discurso sobre as Ciências, 5th ed.* Porto: Afrontamento.

Santos, B. de S. (1992). *O Estado e a Sociedade em Portugal.* Porto: Edições Afrontamento.

Santos, B. de S., ed. (1993). *Portugal: um Retrato Singular.* Porto: Edicões Afrontamento/Centro de Estudos Sociais.

Santos, B. de S. (1994). *Pela Mão de Alice, O Social e o Político na Pós-Modernidade.* Porto: Edições Afrontamento.

II

Theoretical Resources for the Sociology of Education

8

Basil Bernstein and the Sociology for Education

Ana Maria Morais

Basil Bernstein was professor of the Institute of Education of the University of London and director of the Sociological Research Unit. He is among the greatest sociologists of the twentieth century. Bernstein showed a constant and very special interest for education, constituting his ideas the most advanced grammar to understand the present educational systems and the changes they have experienced. He inspired several generations of researchers, educators, and students all over the world. His legacy will keep modelling the way in which we do research and the way in which we understand the social world (Davies, 2001, 1).

Bernstein's published work first appeared in 1958 and he continued to publish up until 2000. The evolution of his ideas appears fundamentally in five volumes referred to collectively as *Class, Codes and Control, I–V*. The first edition of *Volume I* was published in 1971 and the second edition of the last volume in 2000. Bernstein was a constant reviser of his ideas between editions and books. Looking back at his work, he considers (2001a, 371) four of his papers as the benchmarks of the development of his theory:

1971—On the classification and framing of educational knowledge

1981—Codes, modalities and the process of cultural reproduction: A model

1986—On pedagogic discourse

1999—Vertical and horizontal discourse: An essay

He says that the early work in the Sociological Research Unit crystallized in the Classification and Framing paper, where he was able to free himself of the imperfections of the sociolinguistic theorizing, make distinctions between power and control—which he thought were absolutely invaluable and necessary—and show that one could have modalities of elaborated codes. So the question was what were the principles selecting, why a particular modality was institutionalized for particular groups of children.

Although Bernstein considers this a crucial paper, he thought that the most important paper was the Codes, Modalities and the Process of Cultural Reproduction: A Model. Ten years passed between the Classification and Framing paper and the Code Modality paper. He says that this paper looked back and produced a much more formal and conceptually elegant theorizing of codes. The Code Modality paper attempted to remedy earlier deficiencies with respect to the transmission/acquisition process, the defining of context, and macro-micro translations by the development of what was thought to be a more powerful language of description. This paper looked forward to the pedagogic device. Up until the 1980s, the work was directed to an understanding of different principles of pedagogic transmission/acquisition, their generating contexts, and change. These principles were conceptualized as code modalities. However, what was transmitted was not in itself analyzed apart from the classification and framing of the categories of the curriculum.

In the mid-1980s, what was transmitted became the focus of the analysis. A theory of the construction of pedagogic discourse, its distributive, recontextualizing and evaluative rules, and their social basis, was developed: the pedagogic device. The On Pedagogic Discourse paper, first published in 1986, had a much more elegant version in 1990. There a form of analysis was created which distinguished between class fractions and where it was hypothesized that ideological orientation, interests and modes of cultural reproduction would be related to the functions of the agents (symbolic control or economy), field location, and hierarchical position.

However, the *forms* of the discourses, that is, the internal principles of their construction and their social base, were taken for granted and not analyzed. Thus, there was an analysis of modalities of elaborated codes and their generating social contexts, and an analysis of the construction of pedagogic discourse that the modalities of elaborated codes presupposed, but no analysis of the discourses subject to pedagogic transformation (Bernstein, 1999). He provided such an analysis in Vertical and Horizontal Discourse: An Essay.

Bernstein's theory contains two interlinked dimensions, conceptual and methodological, evident in the following two citations:

> [I]t seems to me that sociological theory is very long on metatheory and very short on providing specific principles of description. I shall be concentrating . . . to provide and create models, which can generate specific descriptions. It is my belief that, without these specific descriptions, there is no way in which we can understand the way in which knowledge systems become part of consciousness. (Bernstein, 2000, 3)

[W]e all have models—some are more explicit than others; we all use principles of descriptions—again some are more explicit than others; we all set up criteria to enable us both to produce for ourselves, and to read the descriptions of others—again these criteria may vary in their explicitness. Some of our principles may be quantitative whilst others qualitative. But the problem is fundamentally the same. In the end whose voice is speaking? My preference is to be as explicit as possible. Then at least my voice may be deconstructed. (Bernstein, 2000, 126).

Without losing his identity as a great sociologist, Bernstein made constant links with other areas of knowledge such as psychology, linguistics, anthropology, and epistemology.

My contention is that this is but one of the many reasons why his theory has been widely used across different areas of knowledge. But it is also one of the reasons why many sociologists have not accepted it easily and have criticized it for so long. Their identities have been formed in strongly classified versions of sociology and its weak grammar, and they reject any attempt at blurring the boundaries between disciplines. Many think that Bernstein's work, at which their critique is directed, stopped thirty years ago. But I believe that what lies behind this is much related to the fact that his theory departs from other sociological theories in many crucial aspects, with a very strong conceptual structure that places it within horizontal structures of knowledge with strong grammars and even, I would say, in many aspects within a hierarchical structure of knowledge.

The way that Bernstein developed his theory can be seen as having many features in common with the way theories in experimental sciences have developed. Although this may be considered a nonlegitimate view, it is extremely interesting to think of it within a rationalist perspective, where a model is first constructed and a methodological approach is defined which opens the way for research work, testing, modification, and enlargement. But it is this very feature that is not easily accepted by many sociologists. The power of description, explanation, diagnosis, prediction, and transferability that is part of the greatness of Bernstein's theory is a reason for its rejection by many sociologists who do not share such concerns.

Bernstein's theory opens the way to new perspectives in educational research and created an internal language of description that allows sound and fruitful empirical work.

It is not possible in the limits of this chapter to cover the richness of Bernstein's work. I chose to concentrate on showing how he created a sociology *for* education through a powerful internal language of description that allowed the development of an external language of description to direct empirical research. This chapter focuses on both the conceptual and methodological aspects of the theory. I refer to the work our research group has developed at the level of both the regulative and instructional discourses, with particular emphasis on science education. I also provide a short account of Bernstein's last reflections and directions for future research.

METHODOLOGICAL ASPECTS

Our research methodology is greatly based on Bernstein (2000) and rejects both the analysis of the empirical without an underlying theoretical basis and the use of the theory which does not allow for its transformation on the basis of the empirical. We have developed an external language of description where the theoretical and the empirical are viewed in a dialectic way. The theoretical models, the language of description, and the empirical analysis interact transformatively to lead to greater depth and precision. Our external language of description focuses on the social relations which constitute pedagogic activity. We aim to make some contribution to achieving order in research in the fields of the sociology of education and of education in gen-

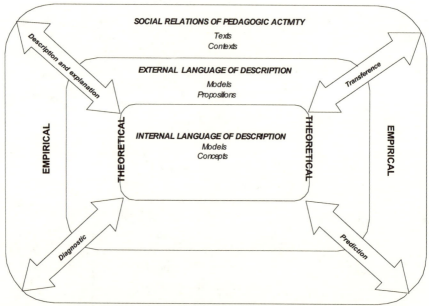

Figure 8.1.   Sociological methodology of research. *Source*: Morais and Neves, 2001.

eral. We believe that the existing "disorder" has been partially responsible for the rejection of sociological approaches by many educators.

Figure 8.1 shows these relations between the components of our research schematically. It entails the following conditions:

- The internal language of description is constituted by a theory or set of theories (in this case Bernstein's theory) which contain concepts and models of a high level of abstraction.
- The external language of description is constituted by propositions and models derived from the internal language of description, now with a higher degree of applicability. It is the external language of description which activates the internal language of description (Bernstein, 2000).
- The internal and external languages of description constitute the theoretical level of the research methodology.
- The social relations of pedagogic activity refer to pedagogic texts and contexts and constitute the empirical level of the research methodology.
- The arrows in the model intend to represent the dialectical relation between the theoretical and the empirical—the internal language of description directs the external language of description and this directs the practical structuring of research and the analysis and interpretation of results. Inversely, the results obtained at the various stages of the empirical work lead to changes of the external language of description, so that its degree of precision is increased. In turn, the external language of description, encompassing changes originated by the empirical, leads to changes of the internal language of description. In this way, the three levels constitute active, dynamic instruments that undertake changes in a real research process.

Whereas orthodox quantitative research has placed the focus on theory, orthodox qualitative research has placed the focus on practice and the empirical. At their extremes, these two research modes are separated by strong classification—*quantitative research* attributes higher status to theory and *qualitative research* attributes higher status to practice and the empirical. The dialectical relation which characterizes the research methodology we have followed intends to weaken this classification, considering both theory and practice to be equally important for sound research in education. However, this dialectical process is only possible when the internal language of description is sufficiently strongly conceptualized to contain the power to diagnose, describe, explain, transfer, and predict. This aspect is also encompassed by the model.

The science of education is a fundamentally horizontal structure of knowledge characterized by weak grammars, that is, a structure of knowledge characterized by parallel languages, produced by various authors and which contains weak power of conceptualization. This fact does not allow for educational theories to originate an external language of description and an empirical activity with sound structuring.

We have constructed external languages of description based on internal languages of description provided by authors from fields as distinct as psychology (for example, Vygotsky), epistemology (Popper), and sociology (Bernstein). However, it is Bernstein's theory which has allowed substantial progress in our research, as a consequence of the power to diagnose, describe, explain, transfer, and predict.

DEVELOPMENT OF AN EXTERNAL LANGUAGE OF DESCRIPTION

Focusing on the distinctive characteristics that constitute and distinguish the specialized form of communication that is realized by pedagogic discourse, Bernstein (1990) constructed a model that seeks to show the multiple and complex relations which intervene in the production and reproduction of such discourse.

The model suggests that the production and reproduction of pedagogic discourse involve extremely dynamic processes. On the one hand, the dominant principles that are conveyed by general regulative discourse reflect positions of conflict rather than stable relationships. On the other hand, there are always potential and real sources of conflict, resistance, and inertia among the political and administrative agents of the official recontextualizing field, among the various agents of the pedagogic recontextualizing field, and between the primary context of the acquirer and the principles and practices of the school. Furthermore, teachers and textbook authors may feel unable or reluctant to reproduce the educational transmission code underlying official pedagogic discourse. It is this dynamic that enables change to take place. According to Bernstein, a pedagogic device which offers greater recontextualizing possibilities through a greater number of fields and contexts involved, and/or a society characterized by a pluralistic political regime, can lead to a higher degree of recontextualizing and, therefore, to greater space for change.

An important aspect of our research concerns the models constructed in various studies to analyze pedagogic contexts and texts. These models made possible analyses at distinct levels and in many situations of learning and interaction. The models also revealed their potential to guide the planning of pedagogic practices and interactions and to evaluate their outcomes. This was made possible by the strong conceptual structure and explanatory power of the theory on which the research is based. The explanatory power of Bernstein's internal language of description has allowed us to use the same concepts in contexts as diverse as family, school, and teacher education to broaden the relationships studied and conceptualize the results at a higher level.

Through the development of a constructive external language of description, based on the relationship between Bernstein's concepts and the data suggested by empirical analyses, we followed a research methodology that made evident the diagnostic, predictive, descriptive, explanatory, and transferability potential of the theory. For example, it has been possible, on the basis of the concepts and relations suggested by the theory, (1) to predict situations of school success or failure on the basis of continuity or discontinuity of relationships between family and school discourses and practices—and also on the basis of the relationship between the characteristics of teachers' pedagogic practice and the acquisition of the recognition and realization rules needed for the production of the instructional and regulative texts required by the school; (2) to describe pedagogic practices in family and school and in teacher training; and (3) to explain reasons associated with families and schools for the success or failure of children from the same and different social groups and variations in the family's coding orientation within lower social groups. It has also been possible to explore the transferability of the theory, for example, when we apply to the analysis of family learning and teacher training contexts the concepts and relations used in the analysis of school learning contexts. The external language of description we have developed has contributed to the activation of Bernstein's internal language.

Our research as a whole has shown how specific power and control relations in classrooms and schools lead to differential access to recognition and realization rules which regulate the multiple contexts of pedagogic interaction. These relations also lead to differences in socioaffective dispositions.

One of the most important conclusions of the research we have conducted refers to pedagogic practices favorable to children's learning, particularly the disadvantaged.

Contrary to what is argued by many progressive educationalists (e.g., Montessori and Klein, cited in Bernstein, 1977, 131), as to the potentialities of a totally invisible pedagogy characterized by weak classifications and framings (as in the case of the open school), our studies so far show that while these weak classifications and framings are an essential condition for learning—at the levels of pacing, hierarchical rules, knowledge relations (interdisciplinary, intradisciplinary, and academic-nonacademic), and relations between spaces—they are less so at the level of selection (at least at the macro level) and, certainly, at the level of evaluation criteria. This conclusion does not support either a return to the traditional education of strong classifications and framings or a total acceptance of progressivism. Rather, it suggests a mixed pedagogy, a prospect suggested by the language of description derived from Bernstein's theory enabling distinction between specific aspects of classroom social contexts, going well beyond the dichotomies of open/closed schools, visible/invisible pedagogies, and discovery learning/reception learning, introducing a dimension of great rigor into research on teachers' pedagogic practices.

We consider that Bernstein's model of pedagogic discourse (Bernstein, 1990, 2000) permits a comprehensive sociological analysis of the processes and relationships, which characterizes curriculum development at the macro and micro levels. It also allows an exploration of the autonomy given to teachers and textbook authors within the educational system. We think teachers and authors ought to be aware that the potentialities and limits of their pedagogic intervention, in terms of innovation, depend on the recontextualizations which can occur at the various levels of the educational system. Teachers are not necessarily only reproducers of the curriculum; they can be curriculum constructors. However, if they are to innovate, they must recognize the context and the possible influences to be taken into account in their activity, critically reflecting on the multiple paths open to them.

BERNSTEIN'S LOOKING FORWARD

Looking forward, in his last writing for the symposium *Towards a Sociology of Pedagogy—The Contribution of Basil Bernstein to Research*, held in Lisbon in June 2000 (Bernstein, 2001a), and in the videoconference that closed it (2001b), Bernstein makes important considerations about analysis of present educational trends and lines for future research.

Considering the new societal mode—the informational society—Bernstein thinks that we are moving into the second totally pedagogized society (TPS), where the state provides the agents and the universities, especially departments of education, provide the discourses. Here the so-called weak state of the global economy is the strong state, for the TPS is state driven and state funded, state focused and state assessed. The state is moving to ensure there is no space or time that is not pedagogized.

The state is making and distributing the possibilities of new pedagogic "knowledges" through a range of formal and informal agencies. There is a circle of pedagogic inflation that does not create autonomy for either trainers or the trained, for both become subject to the targets set by the state. A new cadre of pedagogues with their research projects, recommendations, new discourses, and legitimations is being constructed. This calls out new forms of training and a flood of new journals assist in both professional specialization and central assessment. Publishing houses are quick to ensure that these new professional discourses are served.

Youngsters are to be positioned in flexible time, which translates as being able to be repositioned whenever and wherever external change requires. The management of *short-termism*, that is, where a skill, task, area of work, or the like undergoes change, disappearance, or replacement, where life experiences cannot be based on stable expectations of the future and one's location in it, translates paradoxically into socialization into TPS, via lifelong learning. In discussing democracy in education, Bernstein says that what we are really doing is replacing the word *democracy* by the word *opportunity*.

What is missing in the new discourse is the triumphant silence of the voice of pedagogic discourse. Only by systematically revealing the voice of this silence can we actually make this pedagogy enabling rather than disabling.

Bernstein tells us that he is not against pedagogy itself but he is against the technologizing of the pedagogic; he is against the way in which it is used in its attempt to control. His opposition to what is going on is because pedagogy is simply seen as technology, that a group of people can now put together a discourse aimed at producing changes in individual experiences, knowledges, and competency in a quite, almost, mechanical way. This pedagogy they produce is completely decontextualized, the teaching practice abstracts from the context in which it is realized.

Pedagogy must be meaningful, not simply relevant. The challenge of pedagogy is to put together relevance and meaningfulness, but this is only possible if the regulative discourse that generates it is made explicit.

Bernstein considers that a sociology for pedagogy does not indicate or suggest the conceptual development necessary to grasp the discursive culture for which we are being prepared and operates at too low a level of abstraction to serve as a macro-micro mediator. Looking forward at research in education, Bernstein says:

> What we require today is a conceptually generated systematic description through which the lower levels of past analyses can be integrated and projected on to the wide screen of contemporary change, imaginary and actual. I have lately been attempting what could be called a sociology for the transmission of knowledges.
>
> Such a sociology would focus on the diverse sites, generating both claims for changes in knowledge forms and displacement of and replacement by new forms, creating a new field of knowledge positions, sponsors, designers, and transmitters. (Bernstein, 2001a)

NOTE

This paper contains parts of texts previously published in Morais (2002) and Morais and Neves (2001).

REFERENCES

Bernstein, B. (1971). On the Classification and Framing of Educational Knowledge. In *Knowledge and Control*, ed. M. Young. London: Collier-Macmillan.

———. (1977). *Class, Codes and Control, Vol. III: Towards a Theory of Educational Transmissions (2nd ed.)*. London: Routledge & Kegan Paul.

———. (1981). Codes, Modalities and the Process of Cultural Reproduction: A Model. *Language and Society* 10, 327–63.

———. (1986). On Pedagogic Discourse. *Handbook of Theory and Research for Sociology of Education*, ed. J. G. Richardson. New York: Greenwood Press.

———. (1990). *Class, Codes and Control, Vol. IV: The Structuring of Pedagogic Discourse*. London: Routledge.

———. (1999). Vertical and Horizontal Discourse: An Essay. *British Journal of Sociology of Education* 20, no. 2: 157–73.

———. (2000). *Pedagogy, Symbolic Control, and Identity: Theory, Research, Critique* (rev. ed.). Lanham, MD: Rowman & Littlefield.

———. (2001a). From Pedagogies to Knowledges. In *Towards a Sociology of Pedagogy: The Contribution of Basil Bernstein to Research*, ed. A. Morais, I. Neves, B. Davies, and H. Daniels. New York: Peter Lang.

———. (2001b). Video conference with Basil Bernstein. In *Towards a Sociology of Pedagogy: The Contribution of Basil Bernstein to Research*, ed. A. Morais, I. Neves, B. Davies, and H. Daniels. New York: Peter Lang.

Davies, B. (2001). Introduction in *Towards a Sociology of Pedagogy: The Contribution of Basil Bernstein to Research*, ed. A. Morais, I. Neves, B. Davies, and H. Daniels. New York: Peter Lang.

Morais, A. M. (2002). Basil Bernstein at the Micro Level of the Classroom. In *British Journal of Sociology of Education* 23, no. 4—*Special Issue: Basil Bernstein's Theory of Social Class, Educational Codes, and Social Control*. London: Carfax Publishing.

Morais, A. M., and Neves, I. P. (2001). Pedagogic Social Contexts: Studies for a Sociology of Learning. Chapter 8 in *Towards a Sociology of Pedagogy: The Contribution of Basil Bernstein to Research*, ed. A. Morais, I. Neves, B. Davies, and H. Daniels. New York: Peter Lang.

Neves, I. P., and Morais, A. M. (2001). Texts and contexts in educational systems. Chapter 9 in *Towards a Sociology of Pedagogy: The Contribution of Basil Bernstein to Research*, ed. A. Morais, I. Neves, B. Davies, and H. Daniels. New York: Peter Lang.

9

Sociology of Education or the Education of Sociology? Paulo Freire and the Sociology of Education

José Eustaquio Romão

In many parts of his vast production and discussion of the human being as an individual of the group of species to which we belong, or in other words, thinking about people from an ontological perspective, Paulo Freire suggested, implicitly, the necessity of the extension of the educational discussions to the fields of sociology and history. It means that, even considering the human beings ontologically—therefore incomplete, inconcluded, and unaccomplished[1] beings—Paulo Freire did not forget that we must consider them from historical and sociological points of view.

Here, we must remember that, from a little time ago, there were few voices defending the construction of "bridges" among the scientific disciplines that "sliced" reality.

There is a crisis in the universe of the social sciences. They have crumbled under the height of their own progress. This happened because the accumulation of new knowledge, and the necessity of collective work with intelligent institutional organization has not yet been fully born. Directly or indirectly, the social sciences have also been affected by the differential development of some of its parts, at the same time that they continue to challenge the reactionary humanist tradition, which cannot be a reference today (Braudel, 1972, 7).[2]

In recent decades, there have been efforts to bring together different fields, as a way to overcome the ditches that had been dug among sciences. These ditches are barriers erected as they define their own identities and searched for the legitimation of their own epistemologies through the scientific recognition of their scientific statutes. Each of them looked to setting the limits of its specific power and competencies obstinately; each of them trying to construct the identity of its specific objects, methodologies, and proceedings. In other words, a few years ago, the "scientific guarantee" was gotten from the specific paradigms, from lonely disciplines, from knowledge produced in the interior of frontiers roughly delimited and controlled by truly "epistemological customs."

The opposite movement was also begun, expanding slowly and acquiring academic prestige in the last few years, through the modes of *pluridisciplinarity*, *multidisciplinarity*, *interdisciplinarity*, and *transdisciplinarity*. From this terminological variety to name the collective epistemological effort, we think the last one is the best for a lot of reasons. Among them, we must emphasize two points. First, the *pluri*, *multi*, and *interdisciplinarity* suggest a mere neighborhood among specialized sciences. Second, even though *interdisciplinarity* reveals an interactive intention, it maintains, on the other hand, rigid borders between specialized sciences—that sciences interact but stand on their own territories. *Transdisciplinarity*, on the contrary—besides announcing the interaction of two or more disciplines—translates the inconsistence of the rigid delimitations in the universe of sciences, suggesting that their borders are movable and that they mix among themselves. It reveals at the same time, that a common focus of specific fields of human knowledge is needed in order to avoid epistemological monopolies; these monopolies usually rely on categories that tend to hide or even to cancel out the opposition between scientific fields of study or disciplines. In other words, transdisciplinarity translates better than other correlate words of the scientific world the necessary interaction between two or more disciplines since scientists of different fields of investigation "invade" necessarily foreign scientific territories. All of them have to admit the construction of scientific groups to be successful in their work of focusing the complex and movable reality and analyzing their own changeable representation of that reality. Indeed, these representations are conditioned by the ways of production, circulation, and reception of the epistemological discourses—also changeable because constructed from references of that changeable reality.

Nearly half a century ago, Braudel (1972, 121–52), worried about relationships between history and sociology, emphasizing that dialogical efforts between the two disciplines were limited by that time by isolated attemps of specific sociological and historical production. Saying it another way, when two or more scientists of different fields talked to one another with intentions of approximation, the paradigms were selected by them and they were in interaction. In short, it was not a dialogue between two or among more sciences, but attempts at conversation among them.

Lucien Goldmann studied the relationship between the contemporaneous sociological production and the capitalist and bourgeois society, showing the irrationality either of an asociological history as an ahistorical sociology in detail. Besides this he proves the irrationality of both these sciences when they do not get their references from philosophy.

While composing this work, I initially titled the beginning "Introduction to the Methods of Sociology of the Spirit." After writing it, however, I understood that it didn't fully capture the detail, and that its main question was constructed on relationship between human sciences and philosophy.

As a matter of fact, this is obvious. If philosophy is more than a simple conceptual expression of different views of the world[3] and if, besides its ideological character, it brings also some fundamental truths about relationship among men and between humanity and the universe, then these truths must be the basis of human sciences, mainly as to their methods (Goldmann, 1986, 15).

However, on the one hand, we cannot prescind from philosophy so as not to fall into the trap of scientificism and positivism; on the other hand, philosophy requires historical and sociological analysis of their production. After all, philosophical ideas are also influenced by historical and social conjunctures and are derived from the "views of the world" of their producers, diffusers, and receivers. More than a theory of knowledge, the philosophers are compelled to develop the "histosociology of science" or a "sociohistory of science."

When we focus on the problems and objects of sociology of education, we must know the dialogical efforts that were developed in the broad field of our *mother science*, that is, sociology. It must be observerd too that the more important category of Paulo Freire´s Method—the dialogue—appears already here as a fundamental element to the rescue or construction of an epistemological competence, whose basic principles have their roots in history and sociology. I would like to enhance this instrument (the dialogue) since it was proposed by the organizers of this conference[4] that we should develop a subject with the theme of "A dialogue with . . . Freirians of different scientific tendencies."

So, we now refocus to the discussion about three concepts that Paulo Freire translates in his works with three Portuguese neologisms: incompletude ("incompleteness"), inconclusão ("inconclusion"), and inacabamento ("unaccomplishedness"[5]) from a sociological perspective. Insofar we must search into these human dimensions or "faculties" from the view of societies and, more specifically, from the perspective of the universe of educational systems.

INCOMPLETENESS, INCONCLUSION, AND UNACCOMPLISHEDNESS

First of all, it must be remembered that Paulo Freire considered incompleteness, inconclusion, and unaccomplishedness as common characters of living beings. I think it would not be an exaggeration to extend them to all beings of the universe, living or nonliving. As a matter of fact, aren't we, all of us in the cosmos, despite being living or nonliving, truly incomplete, inconcluded, and unaccomplished beings?

Paulo Freire's thought can be extended to the field of sociology, and more specifically to the field of sociology of education. Freire was not preoccupied with the differences among these three concepts, though we don't believe they are synonymous of each other. Freire sought to keep their semantical specificity as distinct and separated concepts. We understand that it is possible to extract or derive from these three terms, which are apparently synonymous, diverse interpretations about their specific syntax and/or semantical meaning, and how they can be placed in the context of specific societies and particular political and pedagogical projects.

Then let's see the three characteristics that are assigned by Paulo Freire to living beings and consequently to human beings—and that we think are extensive to all creatures, including the nonliving ones. For human beings, different from other creatures, the conscience of those "limits" provokes an incoercible wish to their overcoming. In other words, human beings are equal to all other beings by their inconclusiveness, incompleteness, and unaccomplishedness, although they differ in their perception and consciousness of these three attributes.

Incompleteness

To say that something is incomplete sends us immediately to the idea of complementarity, and prompts us to think about a being that needs to be updated (in the aristotelian sense of this word) and we try to complete his incompleteness, to search for his plenitude he needs another being (male or female), not as an object under his domination and appropriation, but as a subject with whom he will agree to an interaction process that will complete him. And as from an individual perspective as from a social one, incompleteness indicates that the collective dimension is the single possibility of human realization; that the overtaking of individualism is only possible with the setting of a relational matrix, as discussed by Steve Stoer and António Magalhães.[6]

In short, when applied to historical and social organizations, the concept of incompleteness generally suggests the idea that societies will only accept a "universal ethics of human beings" if the outcome of this ethics is the affirmation of individuals themselves, as human beings, without respecting the identity of others as human beings.

Inconclusiveness

The inconclusiveness, for his part, reminds us of the procedural idea; that is, when we say that something is *inconcluded*, immediately we imagine that something is in a process of conclusion, or that it is in evolution. Therefore, different from incompleteness—a word with which it is not synonymous—the word *inconclusion* requires that we think in the process of tranformation by which human beings search for "being more" (human).

Unaccomplishedness

Whenever the two first concepts—incompleteness and inconclusion—remit us to structural positive tendencies (with respect to differences and the evolution process), unaccomplishedness gives us the idea of imperfection, that something lies unfinished, that something did not get to constitute itself completely.

Paulo Freire limited his reasoning about inconclusion and unaccomplishedness. In his last book, he said:

> And here we have arrived at the point from which perhaps we should have departed: the unfinishedness of our being. In fact, this unfinishedness is essential to our human condition. Whenever there is life, there is unfinishedness, through only among women and men it is possible to speak of awareness of unfinishedness. (Freire, 1998, 52)

Here Paulo Freire highlights the singularity of human beings among other beings in the universe. He emphasizes what he considered the distinguishing mark of human beings: their consciousness. However, he distinguished "conscientization" from "making oneself conscientious." This conscientization constitutes the human process of men and women in their personal incorporation in the cultural process. And this dialectical personal insertion in a collective process is made possible by acculturation—which must not be understood here as the classic anthropological process of cultural integration that deprives a person of their own cultural identity. Acculturation for Freire is a process of keeping critical and away from the "animal support" dimension.

CONCLUSION

In just this chapter, it is not possible to provide the detailed focus and give justice to this subject as it deserves: namely, the analysis that Paulo Freire made about our species in the cosmos. He considers that as incomplete, inconcluded, and unfinished human beings are the same as other beings in the universe, and at the same time, for them it is different by their possibility of conscientization about these "limits." His considerations, then, are perhaps the key to the construction of a new epistemological and political paradigm that will help us in the management of our contemporary difficulties.

Reading the chapters of this book, we note that there was one common preoccupation, divided at two levels: on the one hand, it seems that we all come to an epistemological dilemma for the reiterated proclamations about the crisis of the sciences, of the paradigms, and even, as many people are saying, of the concept of paradigm. We are touched by a sentiment of epistemological guilt because our past presumptions have fed so many vanities and so much suffering to humanity. And the salvation, in this case, seems to be in the exorcism of our fundamental truths—not to say fundamentalists truths—through the principle of uncertainty. On the other hand, we are affected by a type of ethnocentric complex of guilt for not having considered the procedural attempts that other people and other social formations tried to outcome incompleteness, inconclusion, and unaccomplishedness that were particular to them in the perspective of Freire's theory. Their answers to the problems and challenges were often destroyed and humanity certainly lost forever the alternatives to a more civilized process.

We do not know how to get out of these two dilemmas: the first derived from the certitude of our own certitudes and the second about the politization of our political guilt. However, Paulo Freire's legacy gives us precious tracks. First, it goes in the direction that the oppressors are the knowledge producers, since he considers them as "the selves" capable of making civilization. Second, he perhaps shows us the unique political solution to humanity: the construction of citizenship of the species into which those who have the potentialities of liberation—exactly the oppressed—have the chance to change themselves into subjects of history, because, as the president of Brazil said recently:[7] "People of the third world do not want to take anything from people of the developed world, but only not be obstructed by them in their historical chances."

NOTES

1. Although the published translation uses the word "unfinishedness," we will use "unaccomplishedness" because it carries the idea of not being finished in detail and with care, which produces a well-finished article, product, or being.

2. Translated by the author from the Brazilian edition.

3. Lucien Goldmann developed the concept of "view of the world" as the privileged class consciousness.

4. Midterm conference on sociology of education, in Lisbon, 2003.

5. See note 1.

6. See this volume's chapter 5 for Magalhães and Stoer's "Europe as a Bazaar: A Contribution to the Analysis of the Reconfiguration of Nation-States and New Forms of 'Living Together,'" which was the keynote of Midterm Conference Europe 2003 — Critical Education & Utopia, September 19, 2003. In their chapter, they discuss the four models of conceptualization/legitimation of difference.

7. In his speech at Davos in 2003.

BIBLIOGRAPHY

Braudel, Fernand. *História e ciências sociais*. Lisboa: Presença, 1972.

Freire, Paulo. *Pedagogy of freedom*; *Ethics, democracy, and civic courage*. Oxford: Rowman & Littlefield. 1998.

Goldmann, Lucien. *Ciências humanas e filosofia*. 10. ed., São Paulo: DIFEL, 1986.

10

Bourdieu's Sociology of Education

Identifying Persistent Inequality, Unmasking Domination, and Fighting Social Reproduction

Patricia M. McDonough and Anne-Marie Nuñez

In January 2002, sociology, and most particularly the sociology of education, lost a major theorist, empiricist, and critic when Pierre Bourdieu died. This essay is at once a critical homage to Bourdieu and a tribute to his impact on the sociology of education, as well as a call to action for theorists and researchers to continue his theoretical and empirical agenda. Vis-à-vis the sociology of education, Bourdieu's considerable oeuvre took as its central focus the role of schools and schooling in the legitimation of the class structure by transforming social distinctions into educational distinctions, the unmasking of the largely hidden educational processes of symbolic domination, the identification of the institutional, societal, and cultural forces that structure class reproduction and oppression, the sociology of the academic profession, and the clarion call for a reflexive sociology that turns back on itself and examines the *doxa* of scientific discourse that unwittingly shapes our perceptions and assumptions (Wacquant, 1989).

This chapter will begin with a brief biography of Bourdieu in order to set the context of who he was and what his contributions are to the sociology of education. We will describe his considerable conceptual apparatus focusing on cultural capital, habitus, practice, improvisation, field, and reflexive sociology and how they have been or could be put to use in sociological studies in education and the academic profession. Finally, we will discuss the common misperceptions of Bourdieu and the opportunities available to us to enhance Bourdieuian sociology as we advance our sociology of education research and practice.

PIERRE BOURDIEU'S INFLUENCE

Bourdieu has been widely acknowledged as one of the most influential and controversial social theorists of the late twentieth century (Johnson, 2002). The International Sociological Association named his book, *Distinction: A Social Critique of the Judgment of Taste*, as one of the twentieth century's ten most important sociological works. *Distinction* has sold more than 100,000 copies in France alone and is also Bourdieu's best known work in America and many other countries. He was even more well-known in Germany than he was in his native France.

Bourdieu authored forty-five books and five hundred articles, certainly a significant social science legacy and one that has been estimated by Loic Wacquant, a leading Bourdieuian scholar, as taking another thirty to fifty years for us to fully develop the implications of his theoretical and research agenda (McLemee, 2002). Bourdieu is the most cited French social scientist in the United States and possibly the world. There are both French and New Zealand web sites devoted solely to keeping track of his extensive publications.

While Bourdieu preferred to be called a *social scientist*, his influence extended to intellectual fields as disparate as anthropology, the arts, history, education, language and communication, sports, philosophy, cultural studies, literary criticism, and ethnography. Bourdieu had wide-ranging impact on academics, political activists, and artists. His influence has been compared to Jean Paul Sartre's in the first half of the twentieth century (Johnson, 2002). *Le Monde*, the major French national daily, postponed publication of its paper in order to put news of his death on the front page (McLemee, 2002). He had long been a major public intellectual, bringing his considerable sociological insights to be sharply critical of urgent national issues like the government's neoliberal policies and globalization (Fowler, 2002). Throughout his career, his work was consistently characterized by this kind of engagement with the struggles and needs of oppressed groups like immigrants, workers, homeless peoples, among others (McLemee, 2002)

Bourdieu was influenced by and engaged critically with many French theorists (Althusser, Sartre, Levi-Strauss, Durkheim, Merleau-Ponty, Aron), members of the Frankfurt School, American and British sociologists like Coleman and Giddens, and earlier German philosophers and sociologists (Weber, Husserl, Heidegger). He eschewed the subject-object dichotomy established by positivists and antipositivists and attempted to transcend this and many other dichotomies like micro/macro, structure/agency, individual/social (Brubaker, 1985).

BOURDIEU'S BACKGROUND

A different but rather important influence was his own personal journey, from his beginnings as the son of the postmaster in a small village in the southwest of France to, at the peak of his career, the chair of sociology at the Collège de France, the premier position in French sociology. Bourdieu's early training was in philosophy at the Ecole Normale Superior, thus, Bourdieu's early years were far from Parisian society and the intellectual and cultural centers of France. This class and spatial marginality (Fowler, 1997), along with his experiences in the French Army serving in Algiers, where he was keenly aware of and transformed by the dynamics of colonization, all laid the foundation for what would become many of his lifelong intellectual contributions. These included gender, marginalization, domination, and his fundamental preoccupation—laying bare how the system of power was maintained through the transmission of the dominant culture, which explains why education and culture are central themes throughout his research career of more than forty years. Also, Bourdieu perpetually struggled with feelings of being an outsider despite his enormous success and this lead him to continuously study intellectuals and the academy.

A fundamental contribution of Bourdieu's almost half-century of pathbreaking conceptual and methodological contributions was in proving the folly and futility of one of sociology's core propositions—that structure and agency are irreconcilable—a dichotomy with its roots in the work of two revered social science scholars Sartre and Levi-Strauss (Horvat, 2001). In fact, Bourdieu made a career of demonstrating that structure and agency are in dialectical relationship with each other and that understanding this intertwining is key to understanding social interaction. In this, as in all of his work, Bourdieu exhibited a thorough commitment to both methodological and theoretical detail and to a working out of his general system of ideas.

A second fundamental contribution of Bourdieu was his painstaking modeling of the social world, developed and refined over four decades in which the micro and the macro worlds are explicated step-by-step, then deconstructed, and then re-envisioned. All this methodological unpacking was in service to his focus on understanding and showing how systems of domination exist, continue, and effortlessly, invisibly reproduce themselves. Bourdieu did this by examining the relationships between social stratification, power, and culture. Thus, Bourdieu's system of ideas about social domination rested on two major systems of social hierarchies:

1. An economic system where position and power are determined by money and property.

2. A cultural or symbolic system where cultural, social, and symbolic capital provides individuals with status and the potential to dominate.

Bourdieu claims that a core dimension of all social life is a struggle for social distinction. Distinction is both a system of dispositions or tastes, and a social space. By *social space* he meant a cultivated embodiment of social distance. *Taste* is acquired cultural competence that is used to legitimize social differences. In Bourdieu's world, we are all trying to use our cultural and symbolic resources and practices to assert and improve our position within competitive hierarchies of domination.

A BOURDIEUIAN CONCEPTUAL FRAMEWORK

Bourdieu's method of analysis is particularly well suited to asking questions regarding the nature and source of persistent inequality of the type that we see in education and in identifying specific moments of domination in the patterns of everyday life. It is especially useful in revealing the power dynamics that support current status arrangements in education. Bourdieu's theoretical framework brings a focus to the dynamics of everyday life and the subtle ways in which codes of distinction serve as a form of power to dominate individuals based on race and class status group patterns. Moreover, unlike other theoretical models, Bourdieu provides a set of conceptual tools that allows researchers to reveal the power dynamics in a given setting and identify moments of domination and reproduction (Lareau and Horvat, 1999). These conceptual tools enable researchers to more accurately understand and more specifically locate instances of domination in social life.

Throughout his scholarly career, Bourdieu remained preoccupied with three fundamental problematics: resolving the structure/agency dichotomy, advancing the practice of reflexive social science, and demonstrating the necessity of always linking theory and empirical research. He believed that sociologists need to address these three tensions in order to accurately and better understand social life.

Bourdieu was "an early and key architect of the widely influential theory of social reproduction" (Swartz, 1997: 191). Social reproduction theory has spawned major advances in the sociology of education by making clear that even though educational expansion has allowed many more individuals and oppressed groups to attend school, in fact, educational institutions have reproduced and heightened social inequalities not attenuated them.

However, Bourdieu differs from some social reproduction theorists in that he did not see education as determined by any group or institution including the economic structure, social classes, or the state. Rather, Bourdieu saw educational systems in modern societies as the most important method for re-producing social inequalities, but that they did so in a complex and indirect way as an autonomous social institution. Thus for Bourdieu, a sociology of education is not a subspecialty of sociology but a foundation for a sociology of power (Swartz, 1997).

The theories of Pierre Bourdieu view the nexus of individuals and institutions by examining the dynamic interaction between individuals and institutions. Bourdieu's theories suggest a framework for understanding how individuals and organizations interact, how dominant groups stay in dominant positions, and how rational, thinking, and goal-directed individuals pursue their own personal interests yet manage to create and recreate social structures.

Bourdieu's theories are based on an economics of exchange where social activity is always and unconsciously directed to the pursuit of social profits and the constant struggle for position, which depends on accumulating, monopolizing, and converting the many forms of capital—economic, symbolic, cultural, and social—as a means of maximizing economic or symbolic profit. *Capital* can be an object or an attribute, possession, relationship, or quality of a person, which is exchanged for goods, services, or esteem. The next section will develop his system of capitals in greater detail.

Bourdieu's own work focused heavily on the stratifications of the system of higher education because of its role in the reproduction of class inequality. He acknowledged that the upper classes invest heavily in education because it has become the basis for social selection. According to Bourdieu, schools reproduced and legitimated the class structure by transforming social distinctions into educational distinctions, which were then socially constructed as distinctions of merit (Bourdieu, 1977b; 1984). What makes education particularly important to study is that education appears to be disinterested in social profits and that this false disinterest adds legitimacy to the resultant inequalities.

The power of Bourdieu's analysis comes from his combination of elements of structuralism with culturalism and his focus on the transformative potential of human agents (Fowler, 1997). According to Bourdieu (1977a; 1977b; 1984), culture supports and codetermines structures, including educational structures, and he suggests looking at the interaction between social structures and a group's perceptions and actions. Moreover, Bourdieu's structural constructivism shows how objective structures bound actors' choice of goals by shaping the way they view their social world. Bourdieu attempts to make the social world more visible by dereifying objective social structures as human-made, but also by showing that the social world is constantly being transformed by agents who are adapting to historically developing conditions.

CAPITALS, HABITUS, PRACTICE, AND FIELDS

Bourdieu's theoretical framework was built on the concepts of cultural capitals, habitus, practice, and fields. Bourdieu focused on a class analysis that is both Durkheimian in its notion of groups who share experiences and Weberian in its notion of collections of actors who struggle to monopolize markets for goods and services. Bourdieu's individuals do not often question the rules; they primarily seek to exploit them for their own advancement. However, Bourdieu's class struggle is one where individuals are all strategists pursuing their own advancement, but their strategies for maintaining or improving their own positions are based on class-based notions of "good" goals and "successful" practices. Thus, "we have aggregates of optimizers, united by habitus, pursuing parallel strategies toward similar, but not collective ends" (DiMaggio, 1979).

Capitals

Dissatisfied with sociological research (like status attainment and other theories) which examined the importance of students' demographic background characteristics and aspirations with respect to educational outcomes and, controlled for variables such as academic achievement, Bourdieu developed a social theory of how social and economic hierarchies were reproduced by introducing his widely influential concept of cultural capital, along with social and symbolic capital. He felt that academic capital and economic capital were insufficient in accounting for these differences in educational outcomes across different types of students.

Bourdieu sought to understand the dynamics of how individual behavior shapes and was shaped by social structures and groups. Bourdieu's conceptual framework of different forms and qualities of capital also emphasized symbolic, cultural, and communicative elements, and microlevel interactions in the social world. These include access to privileged information, participation in social networks, manners in social interactions, presentation of the self to others, use of certain kinds of language or discourse, and appreciation of art and culture (Bourdieu, 1986; Bourdieu and Passeron, 1977).

According to Bourdieu, people maximize status by accumulating and converting five forms of capital for status profit: economic, cultural, academic, social, and symbolic. Capital is specific to these fields. Individuals' constant attempts at securing capital result in structures, which are merely the systematic patterns or ways in which the world is organized. Structures are a social logic organized around struggles for capital. Structures do not mean that individual action is circumscribed, prescribed, or determined. Structures do contribute, however, to tendencies for particular types of action to become established and profitable. Once a lot of actors gain a lot of capital; they change the structures. Pursuit of academic, cultural, social, and symbolic capital is a means to an economic and social power end.

Economic capital

Economic capital is the ownership of financial wealth in all its many forms: stocks, property, and other financial assets. Bourdieuian individuals at best are attempting to secure increasing amounts of financial capital and at least are trying to maintain their current share of economic assets. Also, Bourdieuian individuals are accumulating various other forms of capitals, especially academic social and cultural, in order to convert those capitals into financial capital, that is, occupational payoffs to educational investments.

Cultural capital

To supplement the obvious importance of financial capital and to try to address why students from higher socioeconomic classes consistently attain higher educational outcomes in so-called meritocratic educational systems, Bourdieu conceptualized the existence of cultural and social capital (Bourdieu, 1986; Bourdieu and Passeron, 1977; Wacquant, 1987). Cultural capital consists of attitudes and behaviors that socioeconomically privileged parents, in place of or along with economic capital, pass on to their children in order to maintain or advance their socioeconomic status; these practices act to include or exclude students from different status groups (Bourdieu, 1977b; Lamont and Lareau, 1988). This form of capital includes knowledge, culture, and educational credentials (Swartz, 1997), such as linguistic communication abilities, awareness about cultural practices, information about the schooling system, and possession of educational credentials (Bourdieu, 1986; Harker, Mahar, and Wilkes, 1990; Swartz, 1997). In an educational environment, cultural capital includes attitudes, self-presentation, and behaviors that are used to succeed in school, attain a degree, and pursue an occupation (Bourdieu, 1977b, 1984; Lamont and Lareau, 1988; McDonough, 1997).

Cultural capital is an important form of capital and is often converted into elite educational credentials. Cultural capital is *culturally valued taste* and consumption patterns (for example, prestige or ranking in education). Cultural capital is an important form of capital used to transform aspirations into more valued educational credentials that middle-class and upper-class families transmit to their offspring which substitutes for or supplements the transmission of economic capital as a means of maintaining class status and privilege across generations (Bourdieu, 1977). For example, from the earliest ages students from high socioeconomic status (SES) backgrounds focus on maximizing their schooling opportunities and on using all of their available capital resources to help in that status maximization effort (Lareau, 2000).

Individuals with high cultural capital have clear investment strategies of how much and what kind of schooling they or their children should have. Parents with high cultural capital attempt to secure for their children as prestigious an education as possible because they know it will pay off later in job success and social status.

According to Bourdieu, cultural capital takes three forms: the embodied state, the objectified state, and the institutionalized state (Bourdieu, 1986). The *embodied* state refers to the cultivation of skills valued in social interaction. These qualities include learning foreign languages, developing particular ways of speaking, and appreciating and understanding art. The *objectified* state refers to physical possessions that signal possession of cultural capital, such as books, paintings, or a computer (Bieber, 1989; Bourdieu, 1986; Wacquant, 1987). The *institutionalized* (Bieber, 1989; Bourdieu, 1986), or *certified* state (Wacquant, 1987), refers to the form of cultural capital that includes academic credentials, diplomas, degrees, fellowships, and awards that signify a certain level of intellect or occupationally related skills that have been achieved.

Cultural capital is mediated through both organizations and individuals. Different kinds of school settings offer and expect different amounts and types of cultural capital. For example, in her study of college applicants, McDonough (1997) found that those attending higher SES schools had more access to cultural capital through in-depth counseling and information sharing about college. Over time, individuals build and convert capital in its embodied state to accumulate objectified and institutionalized cultural capital. It is important to emphasize that, for cultural and social resources to become cultural and social capital, they must be used *and* valued in the context in which they are used and converted.

Academic capital is the set of academic and vocational knowledge, skills, and already-accumulated achievements that is evidence of existing success in education. Moreover, that achievement further enhances the ability of individuals to acquire additional educational success or distinction that can then be converted into future occupational success. Bourdieu's academic capital concept grew out of his dissatisfaction with existing human capital frameworks, which he felt did not account for the social and cultural factors that also affect student achievement (Bourdieu, 1986). The acquisition of an educational degree reflects not just the amount of academic skill one has developed in a particular discipline, but also reflects one's cultural and social advantages and the practices used to obtain that degree.

For example, a well-educated parent of a student might advocate for her children to be placed in advanced courses, while a less-educated parent with an equally talented child might not understand how or why to become involved in her child's course placement, and her child might remain in a lower-level course (Useem, 1992). Not being placed in a higher-level course could negatively affect the student's development of skills and impede her achievement, independent of her ability. In turn, her academic achievement could be misconstrued solely as an accumulation of human capital, when in fact it may also be an indicator of the development and use of other forms of cultural and social capital. Bourdieu viewed an educational credential as an indicator of institutionalized cultural capital, in that it symbolically is valued because it indicates that a student has attained a certain level of academic or vocational skill, when in fact, acquisition of the credential also reflects how a student has built cultural and social capital valued by the society in order to get that degree (Bourdieu, 1986).

Social capital

Social capital generally refers to the social network resources (networks, obligations, and relationships) that individuals and families can use for tangible and symbolic profit (Bourdieu, 1986). Social relationships can facilitate the acquisition of social or cultural capital. Bourdieu's focus is on how social capital is differentially developed and distributed among various social classes to reproduce social inequality (Dika and Singh, 2002; Lareau and Horvat, 1999; Stanton-Salazar, 2001; Stanton-Salazar, 2004). Bourdieu, in contrast to other social capital theorists (Coleman, 1988), focuses on social capital in social reproduction of societal hierarchies (Stanton-Salazar, 2004)—and it has commonly come to be operationalized as peers, community members, and educational agents—such as teachers, counselors, or other school personnel—who advise students along their educational paths. These social capital connections transmit information, cultural tastes, and values that are useful to individuals as they are working to maximize their social, occupational, or educational status (Bourdieu and Wacquant, 1992).

Social capital includes relationships with family members, such as older siblings, who can help to ease the academic progress of students (Stanton-Salazar, 1997, 2001). Cultural capital and social capital have sometimes been interpreted as overlapping in meaning, to some extent. However, cultural capital tends to put more emphasis on the information that is helpful to navigate educational and other status systems (Bourdieu, 1986), and social capital emphasizes the actual relationships and relational aspects that help one find this information (e.g., social networks), as well as provide sense of encouragement and motivation (Stanton-Salazar, 1997, 2001).

Bourdieu's introduction of social capital into the lexicon of sociology (1986) was a too-brief treatment that some scholars (Horvat, Weininger, and Lareau, 2003) believe was "imprecise, leaving subsequent researchers free to develop discrepant meanings" (321). Social capital has also been used in some similar, and importantly different, ways by Coleman (1988) and Putnam (1996). Recent cross-theorist analyses have tried to provide conceptual and methodological clarification and specification (Horvat, Weininger, and Lareau, 2003; Lin, 2001). However, an important element in any treatment of a Bourdieuian-based social capital is the inequality that results from the social networks and structural resources that comes from individuals differing locations within the social class system.

Symbolic capital

For Bourdieu, a key task of sociology was to clearly show the subtle ways that social order is maintained by unmasking mechanisms of symbolic domination. As a prime institution for legitimating the unrecognized mechanisms and cultural norms of the higher social classes over lower classes, education was key to his research agenda. In Bourdieu's analysis, social classes and other status groups always struggle to impose a definition of the social world that promotes their interests, and when those definitions (i.e., meritocratic educational ideals) are imposed, the result is symbolic violence.

Symbolic capital includes *culturally valued attributes*—that which is material but is not recognized as such (for example, a person's accent). Symbolic capital is also a set of cultural capitals in relation to each other. In addition, symbolic capital involves the ability of the dominant group in society to assign meaning and value to certain kinds of resources (Bourdieu and Passeron, 1977).

Habitus

Capitals can be converted from one form to another and they only have value when they are activated in contexts in which actors or institutions value the use of those resources. Individuals strategize about how to maximize cultural capital using their habitus, a durable and transposable set of subjective perceptions, thoughts, appreciations, dispositions, and actions that individuals get from their immediate environment. The habitus (1) is time and context specific; (2) is shared by members of the same social class or group; (3) frames individual aspirations, predispositions, and actions; and (4) generates strategies that make possible the achievement of diversified tasks (Bourdieu, 1977a). Habitus results from early class socialization.

Habitus is behavior constrained by practical and strategic considerations as well as by the demands of the moment, and the central role of habitus is in defining and limiting what an actor sees and how it is interpreted. Habitus is a combination of the objective probabilities and the subjective assessments of an individual's chances for mobility. In times of relatively rapid social change, habitus will be mediated by the objective conditions of the material and social environment, and its transposable nature will allow it to be constructed anew in each generation.

Practice

Practice is everyday activity aimed at securing resources. Practice is also the habituated understandings we hold and the way people act. In a Bourdieuian framework, it is what we are trying to explain. Practice derives from an individual's habitus but Bourdieu's individuals are not structurally constrained by predetermined life scripts. Individuals make decisions partially compelled by rules, yet also motivated by creative strategizing and improvisation. Bourdieu transcends structuralism through his focus on individuals' everyday practices, which is a social order of rules mediated by feeling where individuals respond to social imperatives—and not mechanistically, but more on the order of an experienced jazz musician or athletic player. For example, artists, athletes, and other skilled "practitioners" have a feel for their craft such that in the moment of action, they improvise a compelling melody, make the right athletic moves, or finesse an educational decision. This conceptualization of practice avoids the dichotomous standpoint of the forced choice of structuralism in contrast to the free will of unconstrained action. Rather, practice blends rules and improvisation realistically.

Bourdieu is opposed to a structuralist's methodology, which assumes an observer's point of view because it privileges determinism and rule-following, while missing the opportunity to see how individuals constantly take advantage of creative disorder. Rather, Bourdieu's emphasis on actors' understandings focuses on practice, on individual agents' logic in action in everyday decision making. Moreover, Bourdieu's concept of practice transcends rational choice theories' lack of attention to social institutions and presumption that individual consciousness and social structures operate independently of each other. Bourdieu, like Giddens, focuses on the "sheer level of expertise involved in run-of-the-mill human accomplishments" (Fowler, 2002) and that human action always involves complex calculations of rule adherence and creative improvisation.

Fields

Bourdieu's fields are arenas of conflict, and his central task is to focus on the taken for granted and on unmasking the largely hidden relationships of culture, power, and stratification. Cultures are for the most part arbitrary in that each has their own system of beliefs and practices, and many "objective" facts that underpin the system of class domination, that is, merit, are cultural arbitraries that allow one group to impose its definitions on another and thereby maintain its current social position. Thus, Bourdieu's theory and method seek to make clear the ways that systems of domination exist, continue, and effortlessly reproduce themselves. Therefore, a field analysis explains how rational, thinking, and goal-directed individuals pursue their interests yet manage to create and recreate social structure.

Finally, fields are structured by their own histories, internal logics, patterns of recruitment, and reward, as well as by external demands. Fields are constantly transformed by their participants in a dynamic where aggregates of actors gain capital, and then those actors influence and eventually change the structures (McDonough, Ventresca, and Outcalt, 2000).

COMMON MISUNDERSTANDINGS AND MISUSES OF BOURDIEU

One common misunderstanding of Bourdieu is that his focus and, often, his conceptual apparatus only captured the elite experience. In fact, from his first work, *The Algerians*, Bourdieu laid out his argument that in order to understand a system of domination, you need to examine its origins. Throughout this work, Bourdieu identified the social orders of the oppressed, indigenous peoples and the social order of the colonizers. In fact, in most of his work he unmasked the systems of power and each group's stake in perpetuating, however unconsciously, those systems of power. Bourdieu also made clear that education did not create inequalities as much as it reproduced the existing social order.

Another false view of Bourdieu is that he is seen as deterministic. Rather, his overall perspective has been characterized more as nurture than nature (Hayes) because he saw talent and ability not as predetermined but as heavily influenced by investments of time and cultural capital. Related to this issue, Bourdieu is also often seen as a pure structuralist, when in contrast to the structuralism of Levi-Strauss, Bourdieu has always focused on the role of human agency.

Oftentimes, Bourdieu is misappropriated by individuals who have a limited and decontextualized reading of him. For instance, in the United States, many educational researchers have an intuitive sense of Bourdieu's most famous concept, cultural capital, and they try to use it empirically without any knowledge of how inextricably intertwined it is with other capitals, habitus, and field. Cultural capital and its use are not possible without the appropriate habitus, and habitus is always mediated by the field of struggle.

Some Bourdieuian scholars have noted that some incorrect readings of Bourdieu's ideas originated from an ahistorical view of him that resulted from delays in the translation of his work into English (Swartz, 1997). Other scholars have noted that some of the misappropriations have come from fundamental epistemological differences between French and American intellectual traditions (Zolberg, 1999).

One persistent claim of limitation of Bourdieu's work is the limited generalizability of Bourdieu's "French findings" (Gartman, 1991). This perspective could not be more wrong. Bourdieu's empirical French studies are important as theoretical exposition, method, and demonstration of application. One would always expect that the particular findings of cultural practice would be of limited generalization. The generalizable value of Bourdieu is in the theory and method. The cross-cultural translation and application of his conceptual apparatus are always context dependent. It is our job as researchers to apply the theory and method to the specific cultural contexts we know best, and then, to generate our analogs to the "French findings" which will never be institutionalized clones of cultural practice. Rather, we will hopefully find analogous processes of cultural domination and conversions of different forms of cultural and symbolic capitals and particular manifestations of structural inequalities.

OPPORTUNITIES TO FURTHER ENHANCE THE LEGACY OF BOURDIEU

Two of Bourdieu's most important contributions are two of his least known bodies of work: his call for a reflexive stance for sociologists to transcend the limits of their own field and analyze the field of sociology (Bourdieu and Wacquant, 1992; Brubaker, 1993; Zolberg, 1999) and his work on fields of struggle and their increasing development and centrality of it in Bourdieu's later work.

Bourdieu's call for a reflexive sociology demands that every sociological inquiry requires a simultaneous critical reflection on the intellectual and social conditions that make the inquiry possible. He urges us to be reflexive in this way because it is good science and because we have a moral obligation to communicate with others. This latter point of the construction of a critical community of discourse shares a lot with Habermas's ideal speech community (Swartz, 1997). Brubaker also urges us to think about this reflexive task as we develop our professional habitus as sociologists and we develop graduate training and our own disposition for theorizing.

Secondly, there are a few minor directives for further development of Bourdieuian work. Bourdieu himself talks about two kinds of habitus: the first is what is most often used, that is, early class socialization, which establishes a kind of preconscious set of dispositions or matrix of potential actions. However, he also talks about artists and intellectuals and their habiti yet he never specifies how a secondary, more professional habitus is acquired and his discussions of how habitus in general is transformed, other than in response to changing material and historical conditions. This transformation of one's professional habitus is certainly an area that needs further development, and clues to a broader explication of the transformation of a professional habitus may help us to think about the transformation process for early class socialization transformation.

Finally, Bourdieu is very clear that he got much better analytic insight not from comparing the struggles of the poor and the rich but rather from investigating the struggles within the dominant social class. He directs our attention, yet very few researchers have heeded this call, to compare the habitus and practices of the culturally poor yet very rich, and the culturally rich yet less economically endowed members of the dominant class.

BIBLIOGRAPHY

Bieber, J. P. (1989). Cultural capital as an interpretive framework for faculty life. In J. C. Smart (Ed.), *Higher Education: Handbook of theory and research* (Vol. XIV, pp. 367–97). New York: Agathon.

Bourdieu, P. (1977a). Cultural Reproduction and Social Reproduction. In J. Karabel and A. H. Halsey (eds.), *Power and Ideology in Education* (pp. 487–511). New York: Oxford University Press.

———. (1977b). *Outline of a Theory of Practice*. Translated by Richard Nice. Cambridge, UK: Cambridge University Press.

———. (1984). *Distinction*. (R. Nice, Trans.). Cambridge: Harvard University Press. (Original work published in 1979).

———. (1986). The Forms of Capital. In J. G. Richardson (ed.), *Handbook of Theory and Research for the Sociology of Education* (pp. 241–58). New York, NY: Greenwood.

———. (1988a). *Homo Academicus*. Cambridge: Polity Press.

———. (1988b). "Vive la Crise!: For Heterodoxy in Social Science." *Theory and Society* 17: 773–87.

Bourdieu, P., and Passeron, J.-C. (1977). *Reproduction in Education, Society, and Culture*. Beverly Hills, CA: Sage.

Bourdieu, P., and Wacquant, L. (1992). *An Invitation to Reflexive Sociology*. Chicago: University of Chicago Press.

Brubaker, R. (1985). "Rethinking Classical Theory: The Sociological Vision of Pierre Bourdieu." *Theory and Society* 14: 745–75.

———. (1993). In Calhoun, C., LiPuma, E., and Postone, M. (eds.), *Bourdieu: Critical Perspectives* (pp. 212–34). Chicago: University of Chicago Press.

Calhoun, C., LiPuma, E., and Postone, M. (eds.). (1993). *Bourdieu: Critical Perspectives*. Chicago: University of Chicago Press.

Coleman, 1988. Social Capital in the Creation of Human Capital. *American Journal of Sociology* 94 (supp.), S95–S120.

Dika, S. L., and Singh, K. (2002). Applications of Social Capital in Educational Literature: A Critical Synthesis. *Review of Educational Research* 72, no. 1, 31–60.

DiMaggio, P. (1979). "Review Essay: On Pierre Bourdieu." *American Journal of Sociology* 84: 1460–74.

Everett, J. (2002). "Organizational Research and the Praxeology of Pierre Bourdieu." *Organizational Research Methods* 5: 56–80.

Fowler, B. (2002). Obituary: Pierre Bourdieu. *The Independent*. London, UK. February 1.

———. (1997). *Pierre Bourdieu and Cultural Theory: Critical Investigations*. London: Sage Publications.

Gartman, D. (1991). Culture as Class Symbolization or Mass Reification? A Critique of Bourdieu's *Distinction*. *American Journal of Sociology* 97, no. 2: 421–47.

Harker, R., Mahar, C., and Wilkes, C. (eds.). (1990). *An Introduction to the Work of Pierre Bourdieu: The Practice of Theory*. New York: St. Martin's Press.

Horvat, E.M. (2003). "The Interactive Effects of Race and Class in Educational Research: Theoretical Insights from the Work of Pierre Bourdieu." *Penn GSE Perspectives on Urban Education* 2: 1–25.

———. (2001). Understanding Equity and Access in Higher Education: The Potential Contribution of Pierre Bourdieu. *Higher Education: Handbook of Theory and Research* 14: 195–238.

Horvat, E. M., Weininger, E., and A. Lareau. (2003), From Social Ties to Social Capital: Class Differences in the Relations between Schools and Parent Networks. *American Educational Research Journal* 40, no. 2: 319–51.

Johnson, D. (2002). "Obituary: Pierre Bourdieu." In *The Guardian*, retrieved January 28, 2002, from http://books.guardian.co.uk/news/articles/0,6109,640711,00.html

Lamont, M., and Lareau, A. (1988). Cultural Capital: Allusions, Gaps, and Glissandos in Recent Theoretical Developments. *Sociological Theory*, 6, 153–68.

Lareau, A. (2000). *Home Advantage*. Lanham, MD: Rowman & Littlefield.

Lareau, A., and Horvat, E. M. (1999). Moments of social inclusion and exclusion: Race, class, and cultural capital in family-school relationships. *Sociology of Education* 72: 37–53.

Lin, N. (2001). *Social Capital: A Theory of Social Structure and Action*. Cambridge, UK: Cambridge University Press.

McCall, L. (1992). "Does Gender Fit? Bourdieu, Feminism, and Conceptions of Social Order." *Theory and Society* 21: 837–67.

McDonough, P. (1997). *Choosing Colleges: How Schools and Social Class Structure Opportunity.* Albany: State University of New York Press.

McDonough, P. M., Ventresca, M. and C. Outcalt. (2000.) "Field of Dreams: Organizational Field Approaches to Understanding the Transformation of College Access, 1965–1995." *Higher Education: Handbook of Theory and Research* 14: 371–405.

McLemee, S. (2002). "Lois Wacquant Discusses the Influence of Pierre Bourdieu, Who Died Wednesday, and His Last Projects." In *The Chronicle of Higher Education*, retrieved January 25, 2002, from http://chronicle.com/prm/daily/2002/01/2002012503n.htm

Putnam, R. (1996). The strange disappearance of civic America. *The American Prospect* 24: 34–48.

Stanton-Salazar, R. (1997). A Social Capital Framework for Understanding the Socialization of Racial Minority Children and Youth. *Harvard Education Review* 67, 1–39.

———. (2001). *Manufacturing Hope and Despair.* New York: Teachers College Press.

———. (2004). Social Capital among Working-Class Minority Students, *School Connections: U.S. Mexican Youth, Peers, and School Achievement* (pp. 18–38). New York.

Swartz, D. (1997). *Culture & Power: The Sociology of Pierre Bourdieu.* Chicago: University of Chicago Press.

Useem, E. L. (1992). Middle Schools and Math Groups: Parents' Involvement in Children's Placement. *Sociology of Education* 65: 263–79.

Wacquant, L. (1987). Symbolic Violence and the Making of the French Agriculturalist: An Enquiry into Pierre Bourdieu's Sociology. *The Australian and New Zealand Journal of Sociology* 23, no. 1: 65–88.

———. (1989). "Towards a Reflexive Sociology: A Workshop with Pierre Bourdieu." *Sociological Theory* 7: 26–63.

Zolberg, V. (1999). Review of *Culture and Power: The Sociology of Pierre Bourdieu* by David Swartz. *Social Forces* 77, no. 3: 1232–35.

11

Paulo Freire, Education, and Transformative Social Justice Learning

Carlos Alberto Torres

INTRODUCTION: DEMOCRACY AND THE PEDAGAOGY OF THE OPPRESSED

Freire addresses a serious dilemma of democracy, the constitution of demo-cratic citizenship. In the 1960s, he suggested a model of diversity and cross-ing borders in education which became a central tenet in the discussion of transformative social justice learning. As a social, political, and pedagogical practice, transformative social justice learning will take place when people reach a deeper, richer, more textured understanding of themselves and of their world and when they are prepared to act upon this new understanding. Based on the normative assumptions of critical theory that most social exchanges in-volve a relationship of domination and that language constitutes identities, from a meaning making or symbolic perspective, transformative social justice learning attempts to recreate the various theoretical contexts for the examina-tion of rituals, myths, icons, totems, symbols, and taboos in education and so-ciety seeking to understand and transform social agency and structures.

THE CONSTITUTION OF THE DEMOCRATIC CITIZENSHIP: THE PARADOX OF DEMOCRATIC EDUCATION

Freire addresses a serious dilemma of democracy, the constitution of a dem-ocratic citizenship. Second, he advanced in the 1960s, quite early compared with the postmodernist preoccupations of the 1980s, the question of diversity and border crossing in education, central tenets of transformative social jus-tice learning. Freire taught us that domination, aggression, and violence are intrinsic parts of human and social life. Freire argued that few human encounters are exempt of one type of oppression or another; by virtue of race, ethnicity, class, and gender, people tend to be victims or perpetrators of oppression. Thus, for Freire, sexism, racism, and class exploitation are the most salient forms of domination. Yet exploitation and domination exist on other grounds including religious beliefs, political affiliation, national origin, age, size, and physical and intellectual abilities to name just a few.[1]

Starting from a psychology of oppression influenced by psychotherapists like Freud, Jung, Adler, Fanon, and Fromm, Freire developed a pedagogy of the oppressed. With the spirit of the Enlightenment, he believed in education as a means to improve the human condition, confronting the effects of a psychology and a sociology of oppression, contributing ultimately to what he considered the ontological vocation of the human race: humanization. In the introduction to his highly acclaimed *Pedagogy of the Oppressed*, Freire states, "From these pages I hope it is clear my trust in the people, my faith in men and women, and my faith in the creation of a world in which it will be easier to love."[2]

Freire was known as a philosopher and a theoretician of education in the critical perspective; an intellectual who never separated theory from practice. In *Politics and Education,* he forcefully states that "Authoritarism is like necrophilia, while a coherent democratic project is biophilia."[3] It is from this epistemological standpoint that Freire's contribution resonates as the basic foundation for transformative social justice learning. The notion of democracy entails the notion of a democratic citizenship in which agents are active participants in the democratic process, able to choose their representatives as well as to monitor their performance. These are not only political but also pedagogical practices because the construction of the democratic citizen implies the construction of a pedagogic subject. Individuals are not, by nature, themselves, ready to participate in politics. They have to be educated in democratic politics in a number of ways, including normative grounding, ethical behavior, knowledge of the democratic process, and technical performance. The construction of the pedagogic subject is a central conceptual problem, a dilemma of democracy. To put it simply: democracy implies a process of participation where all are considered equal. However, education involves a process whereby the "immature" are brought to identify with the principles and life-forms of the "mature" members of society.

Thus, the process of construction of the democratic pedagogic subject is a process of cultural nurturing, involving cultivating principles of pedagogic and democratic socialization in subjects who are neither tabula rasa in cognitive or ethical terms, nor fully equipped for the exercise of their democratic rights and obligations.[4] Yet in the construction of modern polities, the constitution of a pedagogical democratic subject is predicated on grounds that are, paradoxically, a precondition but also the result of previous experiences and policies of national solidarity (including citizenship, competence building, and collaboration).[5]

A second major contribution of Freire is his thesis advanced in *Pedagogy of the Oppressed*, and reiterated in countless writings, that the pedagogical subjects of the educational process are not homogeneous citizens but culturally diverse individuals. From his notion of cultural diversity, he identified the notion of crossing borders in education suggesting that there is an ethical imperative to cross borders if we attempt to educate for empowerment and not for oppression. Crossing the lines of difference is, indeed, a central dilemma of transformative social justice learning.

How can we define transformative social justice learning from a Freirean perspective? As a social, political, and pedagogical practice, transformative social justice learning will take place when people reach a deeper, richer, more textured and nuanced understanding of themselves and their world. Not in vain Freire always advocated the simultaneous reading of the world and of the word. Based on a key assumption of critical theory that all social relationships involve a relationship of domination, and that language constitutes identities, transformative social justice learning, from a meaning making or symbolic perspective, is an attempt to recreate the various theoretical contexts for the examination of rituals, myths, icons, totems, symbols, and taboos in education and society, an examination of the uneasy dialectic between agency and structure, setting forward a process of transformation.

Language constitutes identities. However, language works through narratives and narrations, themselves which are the product of social constructions of individuals and institutions—social constructions that need to be carefully inspected, both at their normative as well as at their conceptual and analytical levels. From a sociological perspective, transformative social justice learning entails an examination of systems, organizational processes, institutional dynamics, rules, mores, and regulations, including prevailing traditions and customs, that is to say, key structures that by definition reflect human interest.

Though they represent the core of human interests, expressing the dynamics of wealth, power, prestige, and privilege in society, these structures constrain but also enable human agency. Therefore, a model of transformative social justice learning should be based on unveiling the conditions of alienation and exploitation in society. That is, creating the basis for the understanding and comprehension of the roots of social behavior and its implications in culture and nature. This understanding could be enhanced if one considers both the theoretical contributions of Pierre Bourdieu on habitat and habitus, and how social capital impacts and is impacted by the construction of ideology in education.[6] Likewise, one may resort to Basil Bernstein's analysis of class, codes, and controls, which offer, particularly linked to class analysis, a horizontal and a vertical modeling of social interactions in education.[7]

TRANSFORMATIVE SOCIAL JUSTICE LEARNING: FREIRE'S CONTRIBUTIONS

Transformative social justice learning is a teaching-and-learning model that calls on people to develop a process of social and individual conscientization. A process encapsulated in the famous term of *conscientização*, popularized in the 1960s in Brazil by the Bishop of Olinda and Recife Helder Camara. Paulo Freire himself adopted the notion of conscientização at some point in his work calling for a comprehensive challenge to authoritarian and banking education, but he gave up its use when he saw that it was being employed as a ruse to mask the implementation of instrumental rationality under the guise of radical education.[8]

Reclaiming conscientização as a method and substantive proposal for transformative social justice learning entails a model of social analysis and social change that challenges most of the basic articulating principles of capitalism, including frivolous hierarchies, inequalities, and inequities. This poses an interesting contradiction in teachers' training. One may argue that a principle of social organization of schooling in capitalist society is to reproduce the conditions of production of such society, hence how could one advocate and in fact produce social change?[9]

Conscientização is not only a process of social transformation. Conscientização is also an invitation to self-learning and self-transformation in its most spiritual and psychoanalytical meaning. It is a process in which our past may not wholly condition our present. A dynamic process which assumes that by rethinking our past, we can fundamentally gain an understanding of the formation of our own self, the roots of our present condition, and the limits as well as the possibilities of our being a self-in-the-world, reaching the "inedito viable," that powerful concept elaborated by Freire in the 1960s.[10]

Thus conscientização as a process of social introspection and self-reflectivity of researchers, practitioners, and activists invites us to develop a permanent ethical attitude of epistemological and ethical self-vigilance. Conscientização invites us to be agencies of social transformation facing potentially transformable structures. To this extent the notion of dialogue, so well developed in the Freirean opus, becomes an agonic tool of social agency, critically emblematic of its limits and possibilities.

Dialogue appears not only as a pedagogical tool, but also as a method of deconstruction of the way pedagogical and political discourses are constructed.[11] More than thirty years after Freire's main major early books were published,[12] the concept of dialogical education which challenges the positivistic value judgement--empirical judgment distinction appears as a democratic tool for dealing with complex cultural conflicts in the context of unequal and combined development of Latin American education though its applicability in industrial advanced industrial societies could be documented by many experiences.

In summary, Freire's contribution provided us with a pedagogy that expanded our perception of the world, nurtured our commitment to social transformation, illuminated our understanding of the causes and consequences of human suffering, and inspired as well an enlivened ethical and utopic pedagogy for social change. With Freire's death we were left with the memory of his gestures, his passionate voice, his prophetic face accentuated by his long white beard, and with his marvelous books of Socratic dialogue.

As an appreciation and celebration of his work, and his contributions to transformative social justice learning, I would like to quote Paulo Freire himself when he spoke at the University of San Luis, Argentina, in 1996. He remarked:

> [A]s an educator, a politician, and a man who constantly re-thinks his educational praxis, I remain profoundly hopeful. I reject immobilization, apathy, and silence. I said in my last book, which is now being translated in Mexico, that I am not merely hopeful out of capriciousness, but because hope is an imperative of human nature. It is not possible to live in plenitude without hope. Conserve the hope.[13]

A mystique of hope is another fundamental principle of transformative social justice learning.

NOTES

1. In this chapter I focus on transformative social justice learning but I am aware that this construct needs to be enriched reflecting the diversity of oppressive situations.

2. Paulo Freire, *Pedagogy of the Oppressed*. Montevideo, Editorial Tierra Nueva, 1972, page 19.

3. Paulo Freire, *Pedagogy and Politics*. Los Angeles, Latin American Center, 1998, page 56.

4. We are thankful to Walter Feinberg for this suggestion in personal communication to the author.

5. O'Cadiz, M. P., and C. A. Torres. "Literacy, Social Movements, and Class Consciousness: Paths from Freire and the São Paulo Experience." *Anthropology and Education Quarterly* 25, no. 3, 1994; Torres, C. A. *Pedagogia da luta. De la pedagogia do oprimido a la educação publica popular*. São Paulo, Brazil: Cortes Editores and Institute Paulo Freire, 1998; Pilar O'Cadiz, Pía Linquist Wong, and Carlos Alberto Torres. *Democracy and Education. Paulo Freire, Social Movements, and Educational Reform in São Paulo*. Boulder, Colorado: Westview Press, 1998.

6. See Pierre Bourdieu, *La Distinction, critique sociale du jugement*, Minuit, 1979. See also the 30th anniversary edition of Michael Apple, *Ideology and Curriculum*. New York: Routledge, 2003.

7. Basil Bernstein, *Class, Codes and Control* (five volumes). London: Routledge, several years, 1971 through 2000.

8. See Carlos Alberto Torres. *Education, Power and Personal Biography: Dialogues with Critical Educators*. New York: Routledge, 1998.

9. Carlos Alberto Torres, "Schooling in Capitalist America: Theater of the Oppressor or the Oppressed?" In *Promises to Keep: Cultural Studies, Democratic Education, and Public Life*, ed. Dennis Carlson and Greg Dimitriadis. New York: Routledge, 2002, pp. 263–75.

10. Jose Eustaquio Romão aptly distinguished three sociological categories associated to Freire's notion of the "*inédito viable*," *incompletude* (incompleteness), *inclonclusão* (inconclusiveness), and *inacabamento* (unfinishedness). "Pedagogia Sociológica ou Sociología Pedagógica." See chapter 9 in this book. See also Isabel Bohorquez, "Lo inédito Viable en Paulo Freire: Tras el perfil de un sueño." Cordoba, Argentina, unpublished paper, 1999.

11. See Carlos Alberto Torres and Adriana Puiggrós, editors, *Education in Latin America: Comparative Perspectives*. Boulder, CO: Westview, 1996.

12. Paulo Freire, *La educación como práctica de la libertad*, Buenos Aires: Siglo XXI, 1978; *Pedagogía del Oprimido*. Buenos Aires: Siglo XXI, 1978; Carlos Alberto Torres, *Estudios freireanos*. Buenos Aires: Ediciones del Quirquincho, 1994.

13. Various. El grito manso, Paulo Freire en la Universidad de San Luis. Universidad de San Luis, San Luis, Argentina, unpublished manuscript, 1996.

Index

About the Editors and Contributors

EDITORS

António Teodoro is Professor of Sociology of Education and Comparative Education, Lusophone University of Humanities and Technologies in Lisbon. He is past President and past General Secretary of the Portuguese Teachers Union. Dr. Teodoro is Director of the Observatory of Educational Policies and Social Contexts and Editor of *Revista Lusófona de Educação* (Lusophone Journal of Education). He is International Adviser from the Paulo Freire Institute, in Sao Paulo, and cofounder of Portuguese Paulo Freire Institute. He is also the Vice-President of the Research Committee of Sociology of Education, International Sociological Association (ISA). Dr. Teodoro is author and editor of more than twenty books and dozens of articles and chapters published in Portugal, Spain, the United States, and Brazil.

Carlos Alberto Torres is Professor of Social Sciences and Comparative Education, Graduate School of Education and Information Studies, and Director of the Paulo Freire Institute, UCLA. He is past President of the Comparative International Education Society (CIES) and past President of the Research Committee of Sociology of Education, International Sociological Association. Dr. Torres is the author, coauthor, editor, or coeditor of more than fifty books and two hundred articles and chapters. Other titles he has published with Rowman & Littlefield include: *Democracy, Education, and Multiculturalism: Dilemmas of Citizenship in a Global World* (1999); *Comparative Education: The Dialectic of the Global and the Local* (coedited with Robert Arnove, 2003); and *The International Handbook on the Sociology of Education: An International Assessment of New Research and Theory* (coedited with Ari Antikainen, 2002).

CONTRIBUTORS

Roger Dale, University of Auckland/University of Bristol.

Licínio C. Lima, Department of Sociology of Education and Educational Administration, University of Minho, Portugal.

António M. Magalhães, Universidade do Porto, Portugal.

Clementina Marques Cardoso, University of London, Institute of Education.

Patricia M. McDonough, University of California, Los Angeles.

Ana Maria Morais, Department of Education and Center for Educational Research School of Science, University of Lisbon, Portugal.

Anne-Marie Nuñez, Department of Educational Leadership and Policy Studies, University of Texas, San Antonio.

Francisco O. Ramirez, Stanford University.

José Eustaquio Romão, Paulo Freire Institute, São Paulo, Brazil.

Stephen R. Stoer, Universidade do Porto, Portugal.

David F. Suarez, University of Southern California.